SURPRISED BY FAITH

by Dr. Don Bierle

FaithSearch International
12701 Whitewater Dr., STE 150
Minnetonka, MN 55343
USA

Surprised by Faith

Copyright ©2012
Donald A. Bierle

ISBN-13 978-0-9860261-0-2

Published by *FaithSearch* International
12701 Whitewater Dr., STE 150
Minnetonka, MN 55343
U.S.A.

U.S.A. Library of Congress Cataloging-in-Publication Data applied for.

Third edition, revised, September 2012.   9 8 7 6 5 4 3 2 1

TABLE OF CONTENTS

FRONT MATTER

FOREWORD

Since it was first conceived in 1979, and then published in 1992, *Surprised by Faith* and its contents have been read by or presented to over two million people on four continents in fourteen countries throughout the world. It has been translated for publication into sixteen world languages, making its unique cataloging of the extraordinary evidence for the Christian faith available in the heart language of some *three billion people*. **FaithSearch** International has trained and equipped over thirty-seven thousand others to present the material in their own cultural context, thereby further multiplying its influence.

Initially intrigued that the book's content could be effective and popular in other languages and cultures, the author is no longer "surprised" by its apparently universal appeal.

As a result of its broad distribution, over seventy thousand individuals have reported that the material directly impacted their lives and that they have made a personal profession of faith to follow Jesus Christ. These are only the ones we know about–those who have taken the initiative to report to us. This undoubtedly reflects only a fraction of its global impact.

More than a merely religious book, *Surprised by Faith* is also a book of science and of history and of logic. Yet it remains accessible, entertaining and engaging. It stirs the reader's mind to ask important questions. It provides answers based on objective evidence. It uses timeless–as well as timely–scientific and historic evidence. It lays out a logical, sequential and organized case for regarding the New Testament as an objective eyewitness record of the life, ministry, death and resurrection of the historical person of Jesus. Further, it discusses the implications of that life and that account for each person.

As with each of the previous editions, this third edition has been updated to include the latest discoveries as well as new scientific and historic evidence and insights. It has been my privilege to shepherd this important work into your hands in its latest form.

– Rick Wattman
Director of Communications and Publications
FaithSearch International
10 September 2012

PREFACE TO THE THIRD EDITION

It seems only yesterday that I was preparing the Second Edition of *Surprised by Faith*. How could nearly ten years have gone by? That makes about twenty years since the First Edition was published. They have been God-blessed years! This book, together with the **FaithSearch** Discovery event which is derived from it, has prompted thousands to follow the Lord Jesus. There have been many testimonies of lives transformed by the Holy Spirit because of this Gospel with evidence. More than two million people have either read the book or attended the **FaithSearch** Discovery event in the last twenty years.

The durability and timeless nature of the content of *Surprised by Faith* are what have prompted me to prepare yet another edition. It continues to show up in doctors' waiting rooms, Sunday School classes, on college dorm room bookshelves, and even on prison reading carts. After more than two decades in print and one-third million distribution, it continues to be relevant without regard to age, race, culture, nationality or gender.

The deeply gratifying surprise in the last four years is the approval of the material in the book for use in the Russian public secondary schools. The scientific and historical evidence for the Christian faith is now being taught to thousands of Russian high school students–by their own trained teachers!

A disturbing realization has also become apparent in the last decade. For generations, Christianity in the United States has enjoyed a consensus in society: that its message–and the source of that message, the Bible–is true. As a result, there has been little attention given to the reasons which support the Christian truth claims. Christianity in America has become based on the *tradition* of its truth, not a *demonstration* of its truth. Until recently, providing evidence and reasons has been regarded as unnecessary.

Enter the new and aggressive atheists, the prevailing culture of secular humanism and naturalism, the immigration of many who adhere to unfamiliar religions, and an inexplicable bias against Christian faith and practice. Suddenly, it seems, Christian believers must defend their faith. But they no longer know how or have never learned. They find their attempts at communicating their faith both ineffective and frustrating. For them and the younger victims of the prevailing secular culture, *Surprised by Faith* has been antidotal. Indeed, the relevance of this Third Edition for our culture is greater than ever.

The text of the book has been edited and new research added to this edition. Particularly, the manuscript data has been updated. Very few other apologetic resources will report manuscript numbers which are as current. For example, the manuscript numbers for Homer's *Iliad* have been updated from 643 to 1,757; and Caesar's *Gallic Wars* from 10 to 150. Meanwhile, the New Testament manuscript numbers continue to overwhelm every other ancient writing with 5,795 Greek and 24,406 total manuscripts.

A new section in Chapter 4 regarding the "Principles of Faith" has been added. That material from the *FaithSearch* Discovery event has given needed understanding and greater confidence to Christians as they live out their lives in our pluralistic society. While changes have been made throughout, the timeless message of a Christian faith that is reasonable, unique and life-transforming remains the same.

During the ten years of the Second Edition, the Gospel with evidence presented in the book has been established as a ministry in the Philippines, India, Nepal, Russian-speaking countries, and Spanish-speaking countries. New translations have been published. *FaithSearch* International shares the heart of our Lord for the lost of the world, and endeavors to be obedient to His command to tell people about Him everywhere (see Acts 1:8). What a privilege it is to serve the Lord of Lords, and King of Kings! My prayer is that *Surprised by Faith* will continue to serve as a faithful witness until He comes again.

– Dr. Don Bierle
President, *FaithSearch* International
14 August 2012

PREFACE TO THE SECOND EDITION

In a world where change occurs so rapidly that we often stand shaken and in disbelief, it is refreshing and encouraging to find a message that has stability and certainty. It has been eleven years since *Surprised by Faith* was first published. It is astonishing to me that nearly 300 thousand copies have been distributed with a likely readership of two to three times that many.

The repeated theme of reader comments is first and often one of surprise to discover the overwhelming body of scientific and historical evidence supporting the truth of the Christian faith. Indeed, during the last ten years the flow of confirming evidence from archaeology for the New Testament text has actually accelerated. Confidence in the New Testament text and the history of Jesus is far greater than when I first wrote *Surprised by Faith*. I have included some of these new discoveries in this second edition.

Another frequent reader response is joyful gratitude upon experiencing the certainty and reality of God in their lives. For many readers, faith had been an illusive and vague concept. God was about religion, they thought, not a personal relationship. *Surprised by Faith* made the familiar yet often overlooked message of God's love, forgiveness of sin and salvation by grace–manifested through the life, death and resurrection of Jesus Christ–to be real. Faith, then, became for them the path to a life-changing relationship with God.

The need for a book such as *Surprised by Faith* has also increased dramatically in the past decade. The flight from confidence in absolutes and a growing biblical illiteracy has left many floundering for any sense of purpose and meaning in their lives. Fear has filled others' hearts as they contemplate the future. I have personally listened to hundreds of people tell their stories of uncertainty and sometimes despair. In *Surprised by Faith* they have found answers which resulted in a God-caused spiritual transformation, and a new life of peace and hope.

The new surprise for me in the past decade has been the acceptance of *Surprised by Faith* across geographical, language and cultural boundaries. The book has been received with enthusiasm among pastors and people in India, Nepal, The Philippines, Russia and Eastern Europe, and in Central and South America. Countries around the world have expressed interest as a result of my workshop about it at Amsterdam 2000. Hispanic people have responded positively. *Surprised by Faith* has been translated into several world languages, including Hindi, Russian, and Spanish, with more translations forthcoming. It is my sense that God has only begun His work of using *Surprised by Faith*–for His glory!

It is my prayer that this second edition will similarly be used by God in the years ahead, to be an oasis for an often disillusioned and spiritually thirsty society–this time on a global scale. But for this to be, I realize more than ever how important it is to embrace the conviction of the apostle Paul: *"My message and my preaching were not with wise and persuasive words, but with a demonstration of the Spirit's power, so that your faith might not rest on men's wisdom, but on God's power"* (1 Corinthians 2:4-5, NIV).

PREFACE

It seems I have always been in school. Twenty-three years of my life have been spent in formal education from the elementary level through two master's degrees and my doctorate. Now, for thirty years and counting, I have been on the other side of the classroom desk as an academic

dean and professor. The intellectual stimulation of the academic environment has undoubtedly shaped the development of my thinking. I have
always viewed books as wonderfully positive, as treasures to explore. Even
in the one-room, rural school I attended for grades one through eight, I
read nearly every book our teacher could check out of the town library.
Even today I have little sales resistance to the delectable fare served up by
publishers' flyers and catalogs that cross my desk.

It also seems I have always thought about God. Growing up in a family that took seriously its Christian heritage, I had considerable exposure
to religious instruction. But beyond that, in my private thoughts, I recall
often walking along the creek that went through our farm, and wondering
"why" about everything from droughts to the death of my pet dog. A hunger for ultimate answers goes back as far as I can remember. My quest for
meaning was evident even to the old German minister of our church, and
prompted his special visit when I was fourteen to encourage my parents to
have me prepare for the Christian ministry. At the time, and during the
subsequent few years, I did not see "the church" as a source for answers.
The field of science had caught my fascination. It satisfied, for a time and
to some degree, my inquisitiveness about the world and life.

When you add the attribute of competitiveness to the two ingredi-
ents of extensive education and hunger for ultimate answers, you have
the formula for an intense search for purpose. This is the background for
much of the autobiographical material included in this book. Most of my
struggles came during my college and early graduate education. At that
time I turned away from what I perceived as the restrictive intellectual
climate of traditional religion as I understood it. In its place I found the
liberating attitudes of science which I thought held out promise for the
fulfillment I was seeking. During this time I mentally either discarded or
challenged much of traditional Christian teaching about the Bible, creation, Jesus Christ and salvation. I was asking "why," and could not find
the answers. At times I felt there must be something wrong with me since
so many people said they "believed" without needing answers.

I now realize there was nothing wrong with my need for answers, and
that I was not alone. I was also fortunate. At the height of my search I
became acquainted with people who had both asked questions and found
answers. For them, intellect was not the enemy of faith. My encounter
with them established a reasonable foundation for faith that has reset the
direction of my life. Fulfillment had at last come to me.

Many years have passed since then. My understanding of the evidence and reasons in support of the Christian faith has increased significantly. Beginning in the mid-1970s I began to present what I had learned

to groups of interested people meeting in private homes. Since then, hundreds of thousands have attended **FaithSearch** events, many who have been quite skeptical, including agnostics and atheists. My goal has been to create a respectful and non-threatening intellectual environment to investigate faith, including the use of logic and scientific evidence. The most frequent comment I continue to hear from believer and skeptic alike is, "I have never heard of this before! I didn't know there were reasons."

I am writing this book for those who, up to now, have not been as fortunate as I was to find answers. My heart goes out to everyone who cares for truth and the meaning of life but thinks the Christian faith is intellectually unacceptable. I am also concerned for those who have felt frustrated with the inability to communicate the reasons for their faith in terms which make sense to outsiders. In either case, I believe there is help here.

In the writing of the book I have attempted to integrate two distinct elements: (1) a recounting of my personal intellectual struggles and experiences, and (2) subsequent developments in my understanding through research and mature reflection.

I have tried to make the distinction clear throughout. For example, most of the diagrams in the text were added to clarify some aspect of my earlier struggle. Likewise, the insight gained from some of the biblical stories and illustrations came only after later study and reflection. My purpose in adding both to the book is to give the reader a more complete perspective about faith.

The apostle Peter commanded that believers should *"Always be prepared to give an answer to everyone who asks you to give the reason for the hope that you have. But do this with gentleness and respect...."* (1 Peter 3:15, NIV). That's what I have tried to do. I hope it will help some to find the path to faith.

> *I used my wisdom to test all of this. I was determined to be wise, but it was beyond me. How can anyone discover what life means? It is too deep for us, too hard to understand. But I devoted myself to knowledge and study; I was determined to find wisdom and the answers to my questions....*
>
> Ecclesiastes 7:23-25 (paraphrase)

ACKNOWLEDGEMENTS

This book has been in preparation for many years. Not the manuscript, *per se*, but the substance has been tested in thousands of lives for four decades. In the early years, I am grateful for the insightful feedback from the students in my college classes. But it is to the hundreds of thousands in the last thirty years who have attended *FaithSearch* events and classes in homes, churches, and public auditoriums that I dedicate this book. They have questioned, encouraged, dialogued, stimulated, rejoiced, rejected, wept, debated, inspired and otherwise kept my feet on the ground. They are the "flesh and blood" of this book, and my joy.

From the beginning years, I am thankful to John Eagen who played a key role in the development of *FaithSearch* International, then called H.I.S. Ministries.

Three friends read the first edition manuscript: Joel Allen, David Lundstrom and Jake Barnett. I am still grateful for their time and important input. Also, friend and former *FaithSearch* communications director, Nathan Unseth, was indispensable for seeing the original manuscript through to publication. I appreciate the time and encouragement to write that were given me by the Board of Directors of *FaithSearch* International. They are faithful friends. Particularly, one Board member and Chairman, John Parenteau, who was saved through this ministry and then served it for twenty-eight years, was my valued confidant until his untimely death in 2011.

In the last twenty years I have been blessed to have staff and evangelism colleagues who together have helped me take this *FaithSearch* Gospel with evidence message to many countries on four continents. Kristi, Rick, Laura, Oleg, Carlos, Pat, Reuben and Joe–I can never thank you enough for your sacrificial dedication. Publications and communication director Rick Wattman has been a valuable colleague as he continues to leverage his expertise and giftedness to make this and my other publications professional and appealing.

Finally, I owe much to God's special gift to me, my wife, Vernee. She was the all-important catalyst in my becoming a Christian and in my early faith journey. For over fifty years now we have shared life and ministry together. She stays in the background but gives unselfishly day after day to give me courage and motivation to continue on. In a real sense, she is the unsung coauthor of this book.

LIST OF FIGURES

Photo Credits

The author extends his heartfelt thanks to the following gracious photographers and/or providers of the photos used by permission in this book.

Pg. 38: *Magdalen Manuscript*: Used by permission, The President and Fellows of Magdalen College, Oxford

Pg. 45: *James Bone Box*: Courtesy of Biblical Archaeology Society, Washington, D.C.

Pg. 47: *Caesarea Maritima Stone of Pontius Pilate*: Courtesy of Dr. Boyd Seevers

Pg. 48: *Capernaum Synagogue*: Courtesy of Jerry Hawkes at www.HolyLandPhotos.org
Inset: Courtesy of Dr. Carl Rasmussen at www.HolyLandPhotos.org

Pg. 49: *Pool of Siloam*: Courtesy of Dr. Carl Rasmussen at www.HolyLandPhotos.org

Pg. 66: *Peter's Home*: Courtesy of Dr. Boyd Seevers

Pg. 69: *Jesus Boat*: Courtesy of Jerry Hawkes at www.HolyLandPhotos.org
Inset: Courtesy of Dr. Carl Rasmussen at www.HolyLandPhotos.org

Pg. 93: *Temple Mount in Jerusalem*: Courtesy of Dr. Carl Rasmussen at www.HolyLandPhotos.org

Surprised by Faith *"will strengthen your own faith in God, in the reliability of the Bible, and in the truth of Jesus Christ."*

– Dr. Billy Graham

"Simple, concise, and infinitely of value....This book will not disappoint."

– The late Dr. D. James Kennedy, Coral Ridge Ministries

If you have questions concerning this book, please contact us. The content in *Surprised by Faith* is also available in Dr. Bierle's popular event, **FaithSearch** Discovery (see information on page 139). To schedule Dr. Bierle for an event in your area, or for information about his other books, CDs and DVDs, go to www.faithsearch.org or use the contact information below:

FaithSearch International
12701 Whitewater Dr., STE 150
Minnetonka, MN 55343
United States of America
Phone: (952) 401-4501
E-mail: sbf@faithsearch.org

Book updates are available online at:
www.faithsearch.org/SBF-updates

CHAPTER 1

WHY AM I HERE?

The Crisis of Purpose and Meaning
How to Test Whether God Exists

"Death is the ultimate statistic. One out of one dies."
George Bernard Shaw, dramatist

"The certainty of the existence of a God who would give meaning to life has a far greater attraction than the knowledge that without Him one could do evil without being punished. But there is no choice, and that is where the bitterness begins. Confronted with this evil, confronted with death, man from the very depths of his soul cries out for justice."
Albert Camus (*The Rebel*)

Some might question my right to teach about faith because I have not always thought kindly of it. As an athlete at a Midwestern college, I would enjoy the occasional fun we jocks had mocking the religious types on campus. Later, as a graduate student in biology, I cherished the day that a certain religious magazine arrived in another student's office. That occasion became a special time for us scientists in several disciplines to gather for an exposure of the naiveté of people who wrote in such publications.

PERSONAL CARICATURES OF FAITH

During my undergraduate and early graduate studies in the natural sciences, I was cynical about faith and religious people. I viewed faith as anti-intellectual, an excuse for a lack of hard knowledge. Science, on the other hand, dealt with objective truth in the real world. Religious faith was not truth; it was personal preference and opinion. The strongest faith was that which a believer held on to without real evidence, indeed, in spite of evidence to the contrary!

Furthermore, I caricatured faith as an emotion. It was a kind of security blanket for the less informed and insecure. These people used religion to generate a false confidence. But I suspected that it was an illusion. In reality, I thought, there was little substance there.

My third caricature revealed the most about me. I felt that religious faith was a crutch for weak people. My science associates agreed. It was okay if it helped those who were not able to handle life, but as for me, "I was very successful without it, thank you!"

But this view was not entirely adequate. It was unsatisfying and did not provide answers in my struggle with the significant issues of life. I, like others, struggled with questions and fears concerning death, feelings of personal guilt, and an awareness of an ultimate lack of meaning. Clark Pinnock, a contemporary theologian, has written of what I felt at that time:

> We are experiencing... a loss of meaning in our time... According to humanism, for example, a man or a woman comes into the world devoid of any inherent worth, meaning or direction, entirely on their own. There is no larger purposive order in which their lives participate. There is no significance or value for them which they do not create for themselves. They are driven logically to sympathize with Macbeth: "Life is a tale, told by an idiot, full of sound and fury, signifying nothing."[1]

Why was I on planet earth? What significance and value did my life have? Several years ago the musical sensation, the Beatles, asked a similar question:

He's a real nowhere man
Sitting in his nowhere land
Making all his nowhere plans for nobody.

Doesn't have a point of view,
Knows not where he's going to—
Isn't he a bit like you and me?"[2]

The Russian novelist, Tolstoy, put it this way: "What is life for? To die? To kill myself at once? No, I am afraid. To wait for death till it comes? I fear that even more. Then I must live. But what for? In order to die? And I could not escape from that circle."[3] Questions like these led me to a reexamination of the nature of faith. I came to the realization that my perspective was really a caricature–a cartoon distortion of faith, not the real thing.

> *"The question of the meaning and worth of life never becomes more urgent or more agonizing than when we see the final breath leave a body which a moment before was living."*
>
> Carl Jung, psychologist

THE CRISIS OF PURPOSE AND MEANING

Identifying the Problem: A Finite Orphan

Perhaps an illustration would help at this point. Imagine with me that nothing exists–that there is no world, no universe and there are no people. Now let us imagine that some soil appears in this nothingness. It doesn't matter whether we call it soil, chemicals or the periodic chart of the elements.

Figure 1.

What is its purpose? Every affirmative answer to that question assumes the existence of something else; for example, the soil is for growing plants, or as a foundation for trees and buildings. But in this imaginary situation there are no plants or buildings. If soil were truly the only thing that existed, the concept of purpose could not be demonstrated and would be meaningless.

Now visualize grass suddenly appearing on the soil in our imaginary universe. The soil now has a purpose: to grow grass. This creates a new problem, however. In a universe consisting of only dirt and grass, what is the purpose for grass? Some of us would quickly say, "Golf!" Alas, there are no golfers. Others may suggest it is for food or beauty or to enjoy its softness under foot. But in this hypothetical world, nothing

Figure 2.

exists that eats or looks or can enjoy a walk in its thickness. The grass stands alone with the soil.[4]

Alternatively, grass *would* find purpose within the context of a universe which included animals. The grass would exist so animals could eat and live. Then what shall we say for the animals' purpose? To fertilize the grass? As food? Again, for what or whom? In our imaginary world, individual and purposeless animals would die, only to make room for more purposeless animals. We return to our starting point: What is the purpose?

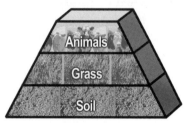

Figure 3.

A significant part of the problem to this point has been that no rational beings are present. Only personal beings with intelligence (rational ability), free will, and emotion would be concerned with making sense out of the imaginary world we have been considering. Dirt, grass and animals do not seek or recognize purpose. What if human beings, capable of rational reflection and having an appreciation of aesthetic values, were to appear in this world (our triangle)?

> *"Life is just a dirty trick, a short journey from nothingness to nothingness."*
> Earnest Hemingway, American novelist

With humankind now in place, some would say that purpose could be realized. The soil would then exist so the grass can grow. The grass would find purpose in providing for the animals. And the soil, grass, and animals would be there so people have meaning and purpose.

What kind of purpose is this? In each person's finite (limited) condition and perspective, the best answer is that he/she exists to "dig in the dirt," "mow the grass," and "care for the animals"–until existence ends in death! Some who die in infancy don't even get to do that.

Everything is temporal and is soon gone. With it goes any inherent worth and significance for our

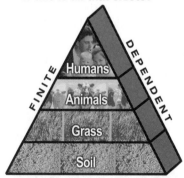

What is the ultimate purpose and meaning for our lives if this is all that exists?

Figure 4.

lives. Is there nothing more? Once again, this was the dilemma Tolstoy's character faced: "What is life for? To die?"

What I came to realize is that this imaginary world I have illustrated is no different from our own. Some claim that our present world of nonliving matter (soil), botanical, and zoological organisms, including humans, is all there is. There is no other intelligent life, they allege, and certainly no God. We are entirely alone in space. If that were true, then all the living beings in our world, including humans, would be cosmic orphans. Pinnock points out the problem well:

> Does everyone in fact feel this drive toward meaning...? How is it that there are those who do not seem to ask this question?... Many... have uncomplicated assumptions about meaning and take a great deal for granted. If life has been good to them, they probably have some personal goals–in their job or marriage–which give them enough satisfaction that the question of deeper meaning seems a bit remote. Unfortunately, however, the realities of life have a way of ganging up on a person with shallow assumptions. Something almost always comes along to shatter the dream and raise the issue of meaning for them...which may come in the form of illness or inflation or the loss of a loved one. There are all manner of threats to the meaning of our lives both internal and external which can conspire to destroy it if it is inadequately grounded.[5]

Illustrating the Problem: A Terminal Disease

This lack of a higher (ultimate) purpose and meaning was illustrated to me recently in a conversation with a friend at a class reunion. When I asked him, "What are you doing now?" he responded at some length but in essence said, "I work." I then asked why he was in that type of work and he responded, "Because it pays well."

"But why choose a vocation for the money?" I asked. "Because I have to live!" he said as he recounted his house and car payments, educational costs and recreational de-

Figure 5.

> *"It's not that I'm afraid to die, I just don't want to be there when it happens..."*
> Woody Allen, film director and comedian

sires. The acid test came with the question, "Why do you live?" After a pause he glibly quipped, "I guess to work." He had gone full circle: His life consists of going to work and receiving a paycheck which he spends. This requires getting up again in the morning to get another paycheck to spend. This continues until some morning he won't show up for work! It has never dawned on many that since some morning they will *not* show up for work, unless their life is related to some greater reality, it has no ultimate significance.

If after death my friend could look back upon his life, he would likely ask, "What was I doing there–and why?" As a high school senior and college student, I once was struggling with a decision about vocational choice. I intuitively felt that I wanted my life to count for something. Most of the advice I got was based on economics: where I could make a good living. I felt that life must ultimately have more value than anticipating a paycheck until one day I didn't show up for work. Otherwise, in terms of the triangle illustration, I was no better off than the dirt, the grass and the animals. At that time in my young life, I did not see any way out of this dilemma.

Constructing A Solution: The Claim That God Exists

It seemed the only people I knew back then who had some sense of peace about this dilemma were religious ones. Their response was, "Don, God is the answer." They believed their life had eternal value because an infinite and personal God explained where they came from, why they were here, and where they would go after death. When I asked how they knew there was a God, they would respond that I just needed to believe in Him without questioning. This only reinforced my view that people of faith and religion were really anti-intellectual. There were no reasons. Evidence, it seemed, had nothing to do with faith.

Wishful Thinking or Objective Reality?

Recently I came across a modern parable that illustrates the struggle I had experienced earlier in my life:

Figure 6.

Once upon a time two explorers came upon a clearing in the jungle. In the clearing were growing many flowers and many weeds. One explorer says, "Some gardener must tend this plot." The other disagrees, "There is no gardener." So they pitch their tents and set a watch. No gardener is ever seen. "But perhaps he is an invisible gardener." So they set up a barbed wire fence. They electrify it. They patrol with bloodhounds... But no shrieks ever suggest that some intruder has received a shock. No movements of the wire ever betray an invisible climber. The bloodhounds never give cry. Yet still the believer is not convinced. "But there is a gardener, invisible, insensible to electric shocks, a gardener who comes secretly to look after the garden which he loves." At last the skeptic despairs, "But what remains of your original assertion? Just how does what you call an invisible, intangible, eternally elusive gardener differ from an imaginary gardener or even from no gardener at all?"[6]

Obviously, former atheist and author of the parable Dr. Antony Flew[7] wanted us to identify the gardener with God and the garden with the world. If God (the circle) is invisible, intangible and eternally elusive from us in the world (the triangle) how can we be sure that God is not just a product of our imagination? If Dr. Flew was right–that there is no God– then we humans would have no ultimate source from which to learn whence we

> "In the form in which men have posed it, the Riddle of the Universe requires a theological answer. Suffering and enjoying, men want to know why they enjoy and to what end they suffer. They see good things and evil things, beautiful things and ugly, and they want to find a reason–a final and absolute reason– why these things should be as they are."
> Aldous Huxley,
> English author

came, why we are here, and what our final destiny is. Said another way, we could not know that our lives have an ultimate purpose and significance which transcends our existence in the finite triangle (from conception to grave). We would be annihilated by death.

Figure 7.

Why am I assuming here that we need to have ultimate purpose and meaning? What if the life we experience in the triangle is grand and we feel no need for anything more? The answer is that we are only exploring the possibility. It doesn't really matter whether someone feels a need for final purpose and meaning. Rather we should ask, "If there really is an ultimate purpose for us both here and beyond the grave, wouldn't we want to know?" An open mind would want to find out the truth–regardless of whether we felt the need for it–especially if the state of our final destiny were to depend on how we respond in this life.

We are considering the possibility that the circle existed before the triangle, and that the circle is infinite and personal–an eternal Being. An imaginary circle (God) would not help. Just to *wish* there is a God would not make Him exist. How could we ever know God is really there, rather than being merely imaginary, created by man's wishful longing?[8]

A Testable Strategy

The answer to me was fairly obvious. If there were a real God, the one way I could know this for certain would be for Him to become visible and tangible–able to be seen, heard, and touched. I wanted to see Him in real history on planet earth. That would also overcome the objection against God in the parable by the atheist Flew. Subsequently, I have come to realize that this line of thinking was appropriate. I see it now in terms of the triangle illustration (above): Is it conceivable that the circle (God) might become visible and tangible within the triangle (finite world) of soil, grass, animals, and people?

> *"If God does not exist... man is in consequence forlorn, for he cannot find anything to depend upon, either within or outside himself."*
>
> Jean Paul Sartre, French existentialist philosopher

Two Essential Characteristics of God

Analysis during the years since my original struggle has given me additional insight. The writings of the late Dr. Francis Schaeffer, philosopher and theologian, have been particularly helpful. He argued that not just any God will do. A God who would be adequate to solve the problem of purpose and meaning, and thereby explain man's personal nature, would have to possess certain characteristics. In particular, two are critical. [9]

1. God must be *infinite*

An infinite and eternal God is one who by definition is complete and entirely perfect, lacking nothing. This God must exist before and outside the finite triangle or I could rightly ask, "What is God's purpose?" Being infinite makes such a question of God meaningless since He is not dependent on anything else. If purpose were not inherent in His being, He would not be infinite and perfect. Likewise, if God were not infinite, He would be of no help in solving the problem of purpose and meaning for us inside the triangle, because He too would be part of the problem. Furthermore, if not infinite Himself, He would be incapable of creating the triangle and placing it in space in the first place.

2. God must be *personal*

Personal beings communicate, build relationships and are capable of love. They have rational, intellectual ability, a free will, and emotions. They are not like the wind, fire, or a radar beam. None of these can make choices, communicate information or reciprocate my affection.

Likewise, the impersonal "Force" of *Star Wars* fame will never suffice for God. It is conceivable to imagine a force (god) which raps everyone on earth alongside the head every day at noon. We would all know that something was really there and everyone would probably be conditioned to "duck" every day at noon. We could be conditioned like Pavlov's dog, but we could not understand why we are being struck (Is it a "love pat" or a punishment?) or how to appease this force's actions. Some form of rational, specified, and clarifying communication would be necessary, and we know that only personal beings are capable of that. A personal being capable of this kind of communication and love could establish a relationship with us. This is not so with a concept of God as a universal, impersonal spirit (like wind or electricity). Only a God who is "someone" rather than "something" could come into the triangle and be seen, touched, and understood.

World Religions on Trial

About nine out of ten people throughout the finite triangle, which is our world, claim to believe in the existence of God. But they certainly do not agree on what He is like. With a broad brush, all the religions can be classified according to their views on the two essential characteristics of God identified above. They fall into three basic categories.

Eastern Thought

Religions such as Buddhism and Hinduism maintain that God is indeed infinite. God is the source and sustainer of all that exists. But the Eastern God is not a personal being. Instead, they say that all is God and God is all. This is

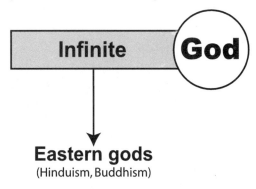

Eastern gods
(Hinduism, Buddhism)

Figure 8.

the basis for New Age teaching that humans are divine since they are part of the "all." However, in Eastern thought about God there is no person there— no rational ability, no emotion, no love, no communication. There is no one to get to know. God is an impersonal, cosmic presence, not someone to see, hear, or touch. God is infinite, yet impersonal, like the wind.

Furthermore, an impersonal God does not provide a basis for discerning moral questions of good and evil. In Hinduism, there is both a good and a bad force. But since "all is God," and "all is one," Mother Teresa and a murderer are both a part of God. In this view, nothing can ultimately be declared right or wrong. There is no absolute.

Also, Hinduism doesn't answer the questions, "Why am I a personal being? Where do self-awareness, self-consciousness and personhood all come from?" The Hindu would answer, "To know God as an impersonal cosmic presence requires that we deny or transcend our own personhood." Chanting "Om" is the pursuit of an altered state of consciousness, an attempt to escape our personhood purposefully, in order to know God, i.e., to become one with the impersonal universe.

Western Thought

The Greeks and Nordic peoples had a different idea. Anyone who has read the mythologies knows that their gods are very personal and

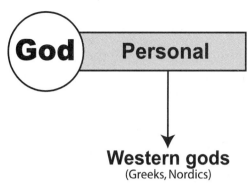

Figure 9.

knowable beings. They have clear personalities. The dilemma is that these gods have more problems than people do. They are not infinite. They fight, lust and envy–demonstrating that they are finite and inadequate in themselves. They cannot provide ultimate purpose and meaning because they are not all powerful and all knowing.

Three Exceptions

What are we to do? The East has religions which claim an infinite God exists, but is not personal (has no intellect, will or emotion). I am to believe such a God exists, but from within the finite triangle in which I exist, I have no way to know such a God; I find that a relationship is impossible.

The West has religions which claim personal gods who are knowable–but are inadequate. The Western gods are not infinite and cannot offer an answer to ultimate purpose and meaning, i.e., how we got here, why we are here, and what is our final destiny.

There are, however, three religions which claim their God is both infinite and personal. Judaism, Christianity, and Islam all teach that

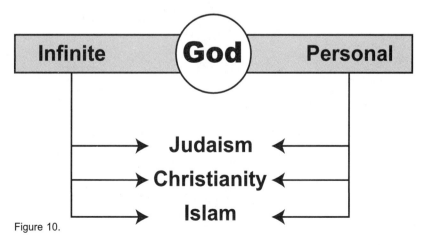

Figure 10.

25

God is both the infinite Creator and a personal Being with rational ability, will, and emotion, who is knowable.

The Critical Difference

How would each of these religions respond to the question, "How can someone know whether your God really exists?"

Judaism would say that God revealed Himself to the prophet Moses with verbal communication detailed in the first five books of the Old Testament (the Pentateuch). Such a specified message could only come from a personal Being with intellect. Furthermore, their God claims in these writings to be eternal and the infinite Creator of the universe. Thus, the Jewish God is believed to be both infinite and personal.

Islam would say the same except that their specified message, the Koran, came through Muhammad. The problem is that both prophets (Moses and Muhammad) claim to get their writings from God, but the writings contradict each other. In order to reconcile these contradictory

Figure 11.

messages, some would say that they are not from God at all–certainly not from the same One–unless we assume that God is either inconsistent or confused! The atheist, Dr. Flew, would still likely object that such an invisible and elusive God could be humanly contrived.

How would Christians answer the same question? Christianity alone goes beyond the belief that God exists and that He communicated with specified messages, to the claim that the infinite and personal God came to earth as a physical man, Jesus Christ. In other words, the circle (God) came into the triangle (world) where He could be seen, heard and touched. For Christians, Dr. Flew's objection is refuted: their God did not remain invisible, intangible, and eternally elusive. Only Christianity claims that its founder, Jesus Christ, is God in the flesh, and not just a prophet or holy man. Because God became a human being and lived for more than thirty years on the earth, He affords everyone a unique opportunity to test this critical difference, that is, to test the Christian answer to how we know that God really exists and who He is.

> "The Christian claim that the whole and only meaning of history before and after Christ rests on the historical appearance of Jesus Christ is a claim so strange, stupendous, and radical that it could not and cannot but contradict and upset the normal historical consciousness of ancient and modern times."
> Karl Lowith, *Meaning in History*

Jesus either *is* or *is not* God, as He Himself and His followers claim Him to be. You don't have to just blindly believe this allegation. You can investigate this person with the same logic and reason that are applied to other historical studies. This is truly a testable claim.

CONDITIONS FOR A REASONABLE TESTING OF THE CLAIM THAT JESUS IS GOD

I wish that my own path in pursuit of God had been this clear to me at the time. Rather, I meandered through books of science, philosophy and religion, trying to find my way. Eventually I did find, in personal experience, the route outlined here. For the reader who is wondering right now if God can be found, I believe I can save you considerable time and frustration. There is hope and excitement ahead for you. Christianity claims that God *has* made Himself available to be known in the natural world of reason and evidence. The allegation that the infinite-personal Creator of the world had become a man, Jesus of Nazareth, is a claim which can be tested. To do so, there are three conditions which must be met.

A Trustworthy First-Century Historical Record

The first condition is readily apparent. The visit by God occurred some two thousand years ago. How can anyone today be sure it really happened and that Jesus was a real person of history? To test this Christian claim would require the existence of written records of Jesus. The only known records which are detailed enough for this test are the writings of the New Testament. My view at the time was that the Gospel accounts of Matthew, Mark, Luke, and John contained legendary stories reworked over the centuries and distorted by translators, so that little remained of authentic history. Indeed, a feature story in *Time* magazine stated that 82% of what the Gospels attribute to Jesus' life and teachings are legends.[10] In other words, I didn't believe the Bible was true. I felt that way even though I had never investigated the literary evidence concerning the New Testament's integrity or its historical reliability.

So the first condition for testing the claim that Jesus was God incarnate is to establish whether a trustworthy, first-century historical record of Jesus exists. How else could anyone reasonably form a firsthand conviction concerning Jesus if they had no eyewitness sources? The first pursuit, then, is to determine whether the New Testament is reliable as a source of first century history.

A Method of Proof

Secondly, in any intellectual pursuit there must be some means of fact gathering. Furthermore, there has to be some agreement on what would constitute an adequate proof of the claim that Jesus is God. The scientific method is clearly the method of choice in observing the natural world. But it requires that the experiment be repeatable in a controlled environment so it can be observed again and again. History is not repeatable and does not lend itself to the scientific method. For that matter, neither do beauty, aesthetic values, nor a host of other subjects. How do you prove something that is a one-time event?

We routinely accept another method of proof for historical events. It is the legal method with our system of courts, judges, and juries. A case of evidence is presented by both the prosecution and the defense concerning the issue being tried. A judge or a jury weighs the evidence and makes a reasonable judgment or decision concerning the issue.

This rational approach to gathering the data and weighing its validity is the way to approach the evidence concerning the New Testament and the person of Jesus. Since the New Testament claims to be an eyewitness document of history, the second condition for testing its claims must be using the legal method. You, the reader, will be both the judge and the jury in declaring a verdict based on the evidence.

> *"I cannot make my peace with the randomness doctrine: I cannot abide the notion of purposelessness and blind chance in nature. And yet I do not know what to put in its place for the quieting of my mind... We talk—some of us anyway—about the absurdity of the human situation, but we do this because we do not know how we fit in, or what we are for."*
> Lewis Thomas, *On the Uncertainty of Science*

An Honest Skepticism

If faith in God is to be more than anti-intellectual and emotion-based, it has to be willing to test biblical claims using the legal method. By these means it is able to scrutinize Christianity's claim that Jesus was the incarnation of God. A third condition must also be in place as well: You, the reader, must be honest and objective with the evidence. The following humorous story of a dishonest skeptic illustrates why this is necessary.

A man unexpectedly began telling his family, neighbors, and co-workers that he was dead. When his wife took him to a local psychiatrist, he was given the task of researching the medical school books and journals until he had a firm conviction on the question, "Do dead people bleed?" After weeks of reading he returned with his verdict: the evidence overwhelmingly led him to conclude that dead people *do not bleed*. The psychiatrist smiled and grabbed a pin he had set aside for this very moment. He mercilessly poked the man's finger, and waited for his response. The man stared at the blood emerging from his finger, turned ashen white and exclaimed, "Dead people *do* bleed!"

That man was not an honest skeptic. Many ask for answers to their questions about faith, answers which are based on facts and evidence. It is equally important that their response to those answers and to that evidence be an honest one. Using the legal method of testing the claim that God became incarnate as a man on planet earth would be futile if one's attitude was, "Don't confuse me with the facts. My mind is already made up."

29

– Focus & Discussion –

1. Can you relate to any of the caricatures about faith mentioned in this chapter? How have caricatures and bad examples of religious people affected your attitudes and personal impressions of faith?

2. What factors, intellectual or otherwise, may cause some people not to believe in God?

3. When everything is going well for people, what kinds of things will they identify as satisfying their need for purpose and meaning?

4. Muslims and Jews claim to know God through messages He gave to prophets, while Christians claim to know God because He also walked the earth as a human. Why is the difference in these two views significant when it comes to testing for the existence of God?

5. Which can be used in a court of law: an eyewitness account or hearsay? Why? How is this important to the first condition identified as necessary to test legally the claim that Jesus is God?

6. Do you agree that the validity of the Christian faith can be explored rationally? Why or why not?

– DISCOVERIES –

What you have read in Chapter 1 can be summarized in two discoveries, what I call *"Ah-ha!"* discoveries.

1. Death is the ultimate and final conqueror if the finite world is all there is!

2. Christianity alone claims we can know God exists because He came to earth physically as the man Jesus Christ two thousand years ago!

WHAT'S NEXT?

I said in this chapter that the objective way to know whether God exists (and who He is) would be for Him to come physically to earth where He could be seen, heard, and touched. Christianity says that's *exactly what He did* in the person of Jesus.

Is the Christian claim true? One of the conditions for testing the claim is the existence of records from eyewitnesses which tell what Jesus said and did when He was on earth. Do such records exist? How can we know they are trustworthy? These are the discoveries we will make in the next chapter.

CHAPTER 2

IS THE BIBLE TRUE?

The Tests of Integrity and Historical Reliability

"The historical Bible (the written Word) and Jesus Christ (the living Word) are the two cornerstones of the Christian worldview. If the Bible is not history or if Jesus Christ is not 'God with us' (Matthew 1:23), Christianity crumbles. To shatter Christian doctrine and the Christian worldview, one need only shatter its historical underpinnings..."
David A. Noebel (*Understanding the Times*)

࿇

"The test of truth is the known factual evidence..."
Jacob Bronowski (*Science and Human Values*)

The most foundational and unique truth claim of Christianity is that Jesus Christ was God in human flesh, the highest, most illuminating revelation of God to man. It is further claimed that Jesus revealed to all who knew Him, by what He said and did, that He was the unique Son of God. This is what we want to test.

The difficulty is not in recognizing the historical reality of a man called Jesus of Nazareth, for that is assured by several recognized extrabiblical sources.[1] Historical research scholar, Dr. Edwin Yamauchi, sets the record straight on this: "From time to time some people have tried to deny the existence of Jesus, but this is really a lost cause... There is overwhelming evidence that Jesus did exist..."[2] The real difficulty for some is that the only detailed biography of this man Jesus is in the biblical Gospel sources of Matthew, Mark, Luke, and John. Are these records credible, i.e., are they an authentic and historically reliable record of the words and deeds of Jesus?

A serious, yet amusing, commentary on this question was written to syndicated columnist, Ann Landers. It is extreme in its wording, but not unique in the opinion expressed.

Dear Ann: Please, for heaven's sake, stop pushing religion! Anyone with half a brain knows that your readers are, for the most part, simple-minded, superstitious dimwits who can't face life without a crutch. But doesn't it bother you when you advise about the laws of God–a 2,000-year-old fairy tale? One day I hope you write a column denouncing the God myth and then quit! The ultimate limit of human foolishness, the most preposterous bit of irrational hokum ever dreamed up by humankind is the baloney found in the scriptures. Such nonsense is for weaklings and idiots who are unable to think for themselves or accept responsibility for their own actions.[3]

If this commentary were valid, there would be little hope of forming a reasonable and objective personal conviction concerning the claim that Jesus is God. Is this writer's position supported by evidence?

TESTING THE INTEGRITY OF THE NEW TESTAMENT

The testing of ancient documents for integrity is a common practice among literary scholars. There is a large body of literature, written both earlier and later than the New Testament, where integrity is also an issue. For example, the histories of Herodotus and Caesar (fifth and first centuries B.C., respectively) are well known. Tacitus and Josephus wrote histories of Rome and of the Jews, respectively, about the end of the first century A.D. The criteria for testing such literature for integrity are well established among scholars. Therefore, there is no need to create anything new for examination of the New Testament writings. We need only to apply already accepted criteria.

Because this is unfamiliar ground for most, it is necessary to imagine an ancient scenario to understand the issues. There is a well-known work written about 50 B.C. entitled *The Gallic Wars*.[4] These are the personal memoirs of Roman Emperor Julius Caesar's military campaigns. Let us suppose shortly after they were written that a friend of Julius was visiting the palace, noted the work, and requested a copy for his own library. Julius would have granted his request, but there was no scanner or photocopier in his office, and no digital copy to send attached to an E-mail, or to post on Facebook, or to his personal blog. Instead, the friend would have needed to send for a trained copyist who would labor for weeks to handwrite every letter, word and sentence. Would the copy be exactly like the Emperor's original? That is unlikely.

Now imagine that a person visits the home of Julius' friend, notes his copy of *The Gallic Wars,* and secures permission to have his own copyist come in to make a second generation copy for himself. Will it be exactly like the first generation copy? That is also unlikely. It will likely have even more changes from the Emperor's original. To the extent that changes occur in the copies, is the extent to which the work has lost some of its integrity. So far the changes are probably minor, but multiply that scenario by hundreds of generations over centuries of time. The integrity is certain to degenerate. By the time we reach the fifteenth century and put the copies of that generation onto Gutenberg's newly-invented printing press, it is possible that only a part of the Caesar's original writing may remain.

Why not just refer back to the Emperor's original writing? Why rely on copies at all if we can go to the autograph (the handwritten original)? The answer is simple: there are no autographs. Not only has no original of *The Gallic Wars* ever been found; neither have the autographs of Aristotle, Muhammad or any other ancient writer. Therefore, even with the New Testament, we must work from whatever scribal copies have been found. This requires the development of some guidelines for determining the degree of integrity for the current text.

Three Questions

The test of integrity determines whether the New Testament Gospels originated in the eyewitness generation of Jesus, and whether these accounts were transmitted to us over the centuries without major changes. Specifically, we need to know if the twenty-first century English New Testament is a reasonably accurate reproduction of the original first-century Greek New Testament. There are three primary questions scholars ask of ancient literature to determine this.

1. How Many Manuscripts Have Been Found?

The first question concerns the number of handwritten copies which have been found, that is, the manuscript evidence. The more abundant the number of ancient copies that are found, the better. Even if there are variant readings, a large number of copies allows comparison and correlation in order to more accurately restore the original text. Furthermore, a large number of manuscripts over the centuries minimizes the possibility that a little band of people fraudulently fabricated the documents "behind closed doors," so to speak. A large number of copies means broader public exposure and greater accountability to integrity.

As a youth I knew virtually nothing about manuscript studies. My first exposure, though quite limited, came during college. In my skepticism, I remember thinking that it was probably certain that the New Testament evidence would be quite inferior to evidence supporting the writings of the great classical writers such as Plato, Homer or Aristotle. Later in graduate school I discovered, to my surprise, that the New Testament is vastly superior. Additional study over the years has enhanced my understanding of this academic discipline. These later insights are included throughout this chapter to give the reader a more thorough understanding of the evidence for the first condition needed to test the Christian claim about Jesus.

How many manuscript copies of ancient works are available for study today?[5,6] Obviously, to know a work existed we would need to have found at least one.[7] The 1,757 existing manuscript copies of Homer's *Iliad* offer an exceptional example among ancient works. Most have manuscript copies numbering only in the single, double, or low triple digits. There are only about 251 manuscripts ever found of Caesar's *The Gallic Wars*, 210 for Plato's Tetralogies, 150 for Livy's *History of Rome* (*Ab Urbe Condita*) and only 33 for Tacitus' minor works (31 of those are from the fifteenth century).

What about the New Testament? There are 5,795 known manuscripts in the original Greek language.[8] There are, in addition, some 18,611 ancient New Testament manuscripts in Latin, Coptic, Syriac, Ethiopian, Armenian, and other language versions, together with New Testament text found in ancient hymn books (lectionaries) of the early church.[9] Added together with the Greek manuscripts, about 24,406 scribal copies of portions or all of the New Testament have survived. British scholar F.F. Bruce concludes from the data, "There is no body of ancient literature in the world which enjoys such a wealth of good textual attestation as the New Testament."[10] Figure 1 shows the extreme contrast between the manuscript evidence for the New Testament and that of other selected ancient writings.

The comparison is not even close. So much for my reasonable certainty that the New Testament would not fare well under scholarly

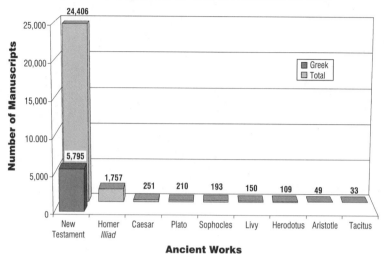

The Number of New Testament Manuscripts Compared to Other Ancient Works

Figure 1.

scrutiny! When my reading during graduate school exposed me to these facts, I realized I had been dishonest. I never questioned, or even examined, the accuracy of the ancient texts of other works I had read. Yet somehow I *knew* the New Testament text could not be trusted, and feigned intellectual reasons for my distrust. However, my ignorance was the real culprit. Later in my career, when reading Sir Frederic Kenyon, the eminent scholar of textual criticism, I found out that I had not been alone in holding this double standard:

> Scholars are satisfied that they possess substantially the true text of the principal Greek and Roman writers whose works have come down to us, of Sophocles, of Thucydides, of Cicero, of Virgil; yet our knowledge of their writings depends on a mere handful of manuscripts, whereas the manuscripts of the New Testament are counted by hundreds, and even thousands.[11]

2. How Early Are The Manuscripts?

The second issue affecting integrity is the date when the discovered manuscripts had been produced by the scribe. Obviously, the further removed in time the copies are from the originals, the more likely they are to have accumulated copyist errors, additions, and deletions, i.e., to

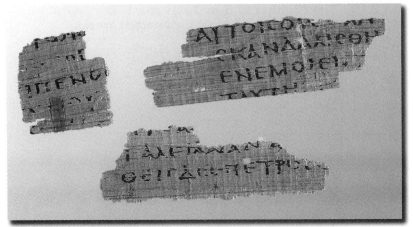

Used by permission. The President and Fellows of Magdalen College, Oxford

MAGDALEN MANUSCRIPT
Allegedly the oldest known manuscript of the New Testament–a fragment of Matthew 26. Dated by papyrologist Dr. Carsten Peter Thiede at about A.D. 60.

have less integrity. Fortunately, while the total number of these errors is greater simply because of the large number of New Testament manuscripts, the large number of manuscripts also increases proportionately the means for detecting such errors and restoring the original wording.

How close to the authorship do archaeologists actually find ancient manuscript copies? Julius Caesar's *The Gallic Wars* was authored about 50 B.C., yet we have no manuscripts available for study today which were copied before the ninth century–a gap of some 950 years. This is not unusual since the gap between authorship and the first known manuscript for most of the Greek and Latin works varies from about 400-1,450 years.[12] The short spans of Sophocles (200 years) and Virgil (300 years) are extremely unusual. Such a short time period is not at all typical. People are troubled when they discover that there are no preserved copies of most classical works for hundreds of years after the date of original composition. But they are astonished when they see the data concerning the New Testament.

It is generally agreed that the twenty-seven books and letters of the New Testament were penned over a 50-year period, beginning approximately A.D. 47. For ease in calculations, I will use the year A.D. 100 as the latest possible date for their completion. What is the earliest copy ever found? Remember, the range for all other literature is 200 to about 1,500 years after authorship. The John Rylands papyrus, designated by scholars as P52, is a fragment containing a few verses of the New Testament Gospel of John, dating about A.D. 125. This is only some 35 years after the original Gospel had been written by the apostle. Whoever used this copy could have known the author, or even been personally taught by the apostle John himself.

Furthermore, a strong case has been made recently by Dr. Young Kyu Kim, a manuscript scholar, that the Chester Beatty Papyrus (P46) containing all of Paul's epistles except the pastorals (First and Second Timothy, and Titus) should be redated to the late first century. This is only about 20 years after the apostle died![13]

That's not all. Studies of the writings of the Apostolic Fathers from about A.D. 95-110 (they were students of the eyewitness apostles of Jesus) like Polycarp, Clement of Rome, and Ignatius, reveal extensive quoting of the New Testament. For example, about A.D. 96, Clement of Rome referred to the Gospels of Matthew, Mark, and Luke, and eight other New Testament letters. They are quoted as if the readers were fully aware of them, suggesting these New Testament books must have been written some time earlier in the first century.[14]

Supporting that conclusion are the recently analyzed fragments of Matthew (Magdalen Papyrus); a scroll fragment of Mark at Qumran; and a papyrus fragment of Luke in a Paris library. These have been dated by some scholars between A.D. 50 and A.D. 70.[15] In February, 2012, Daniel Wallace reported a new papyrus of the Gospel of Mark which one of the world's leading paleographers said was certainly from the first century. It is scheduled to be published in 2013.[16] Since Jesus lived at least until A.D. 30, these copies were made by people who were contemporaries of Jesus–people who knew Him personally or talked with those who did. While these manuscripts are all fragments and their exact dates are still to be determined, they nevertheless demonstrate that *the Gospels were in written form very early*. They did *not* go through a long period of oral transmission during which they would have taken on legendary traditions. *No other ancient writing* can trace its manuscript copies all the way back to the generation of the eyewitnesses and its original authors! The New Testament is unique in its manuscript integrity.

However, a find consisting of more-complete Gospels would be needed to do textual studies. The Bodmer and Chester Beatty papyri, dating from about A.D. 150-220, exceed every demand in this regard. Manuscripts designated P45, P66, and P75 contain complete copies of the Gospels, including the miracles of Jesus and the details of His resurrection, and were copied within 100 years of the originals.[17] Kenyon's commentary on the significance of these manuscripts contradicts many people's perception of what is true regarding the New Testament records.

The net result of this discovery... is, in fact, to reduce the gap between the earlier manuscripts and the traditional dates of the New Testament books so far that it becomes negligible in any discussion of their authenticity. No other ancient book has anything like such early and plentiful testimony to its text, and no unbiased scholar would deny that the text that has come down to us is substantially sound.[18]

Figure 2 (below) compares several ancient works with the New Testament in regard to the time interval between the original authorship and the earliest extant copies.

Again, the New Testament stands far above all other ancient writings in both the number of manuscripts and the short time span between authorship and the earliest extant copies. There is a nearly continuous chain of copies from the time of the first-century originals to the fifteenth-century printing press. If anyone wants to allege that the text of the New Testament we have today is not essentially like the original autographs, they must first answer, "When could they possibly have become corrupted?"

Recent research on the longevity of ancient books may make any remaining gap between the autographs and the first surviving New Testament manuscripts a moot point. Ancients used manuscripts any-

The Time Interval Between the Date of Writing and the Earliest Known Manuscript of the New Testament Compared to Other Ancient Works

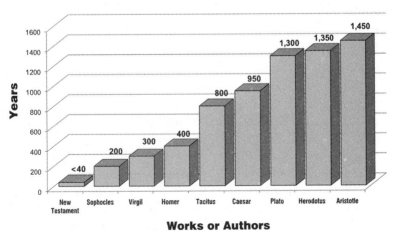

Figure 2.

where from 150-500 years before they were discarded. This has profound implications according to scholar Craig Evans: "If the first-century originals, or 'autographs' of the Gospels continued in use for 150 years or more, they would still have been in circulation when the oldest copies of the Gospels that we possess today were copied."[19]

Furthermore, recent evidence reveals that ancient documents were almost always prepared in duplicate before the original was sent out. Evans states: "In effect this factor 'doubles' the chances of first-century originals surviving well into the second century and perhaps into the third, thus overlapping with our oldest extant manuscripts."[20]

Based on this evidence, the conclusion of scholar F.F. Bruce is certainly justified:

> The evidence for our New Testament writings is ever so much greater than the evidence for many writings of classical authors, the authenticity of which no-one dreams of questioning. And if the New Testament were a collection of secular writings, their authenticity would generally be regarded as beyond all doubt.[21]

3. How Accurately Were The Manuscripts Copied?

The final question measures the extent of distortion of the text due to copying over the centuries. I have already shared the history of my former contention that the text of the New Testament must have been quite significantly muddled by insertions, interpretations, and translation. Scholars refer to this as distortion of the meaning of the text. Several people reading such diverse manuscripts would necessarily arrive at different understandings.

Dr. Bruce Metzger, professor of New Testament language and literature at Princeton, published an analysis on this very question. He compared research into the many manuscripts of three ancient works: Homer's *Iliad*, a religious work of the ancient Greeks; the *Mahabharata*, a religious book of Hinduism; and the Christian New Testament.[22] The works varied in length from 15,600 lines for the *Iliad*; 20,000 for the New Testament; and 250,000 for the *Mahabharata*. Variations such as spelling differences, word order, etc., which did not affect the meaning of the text, were ignored. All differences in the manuscripts affecting the reader's understanding were counted. How much distortion did he find?

Dr. Metzger summarized that 764 lines of the *Iliad* were corrupted, a distortion rate of about 5%. Said another way, the meaning of one out of every twenty lines is uncertain. Which *Iliad* do we read in literature class? Who decided which ancient manuscript was the correct one? Yet, it is probably rare that an instructor would caution students about the integrity of the *Iliad* when it is assigned or discussed in class. Its integrity is assumed without question.

The *Mahabharata* was even worse with at least 26,000 lines corrupted, somewhat more than a 10% distortion rate. One out of every ten lines of this religious book is "up for grabs," so to speak. This is not a very reliable source on which to base your life or destiny!

The data for the New Testament, on the other hand, is incredible. Only 40 of 20,000 lines, or 1/5 of 1% (0.2%) are distorted.[23] This is 1/25 of the distortion found in the *Iliad*, which itself has a low distortion rate among ancient writings. Further, F.F. Bruce has said that "the variant readings about which any doubt remains among textual critics of the New Testament affect no material question of historic fact or of Christian faith and practice."[24] Said more simply, no teaching of the Christian faith is in question as a result of the minor distortions of the New Testament text due to copying over many centuries. Where was the textual confusion which I felt made the New Testament so unacceptable to me during my college years? Figure 3 (below) summarizes Metzger's analysis.

A Comparison of the Rate of Distortion of Manuscripts Due to Copying Errors

Figure 3.

The Evidence of New Testament Quotes in Other Ancient Writings

There is an additional strong argument for the integrity of the New Testament. The extant writings of the church fathers of the first three centuries after Christ contain over 36,000 quotations or allusions to New Testament books.[25] Metzger and Ehrman comment about the significance of this:

> Besides textual evidence derived from New Testament Greek manuscripts and from early versions, the textual critic has available the numerous scriptural quotations included in the commentaries, sermons, and other treatises written by the early Church fathers. Indeed, so extensive are these citations that if all other sources for our knowledge of the text of the New Testament were destroyed they would be sufficient alone for the reconstruction of practically the entire New Testament.[26]

Textual scholar Kenyon states this truth another way:

> It cannot be too strongly asserted that in substance the text of the Bible is certain: Especially is this the case with the New Testament. The number of manuscripts of the New Testament, of early translations from it, and of quotations from it in the oldest writers of the Church, is so large that it is practically certain that the true reading of every doubtful passage is preserved in some one or other of these ancient authorities. This can be said of no other ancient book in the world.[27]

The weight of this evidence would have been very significant for me when I was wrestling with these issues. Unfortunately, at that time I didn't know about it. But it was exposure to this evidence during graduate school that began a revolution in my thinking. Subsequently, I have become persuaded that when I pick up my current copy of the New Testament records of Jesus' life, it is essentially the same as when the eyewitnesses wrote it two thousand years ago in the first century A.D. This was the earlier conclusion of researcher and scholar Kenyon:

> ...[T]he last foundation for any doubt that the Scriptures have come down to us substantially as they were written has

now been removed. Both the authenticity and the general integrity of the books of the New Testament may be regarded as finally established.[28]

How can someone know whether what the first-century writers wrote is true? Maybe Matthew liked to write fairy tales. Just because we have an authentic record of the first-century New Testament writings doesn't guarantee that it is history. It could be myth. So far I have only demonstrated that the New Testament text has greater integrity compared with all other ancient writings because it: 1) has more manuscripts; 2) has earlier manuscripts; and 3) is more-accurately copied. How can a person today know whether what the original authors wrote about *really happened* as they described it?

TESTING THE HISTORICAL RELIABILITY OF THE NEW TESTAMENT

Testing the truthfulness of the New Testament records requires some independent sources which would substantiate its historical accuracy. There is also a need to learn more about the New Testament documents and their authors within the historical context of the first century. Are the documents internally consistent? These are issues addressed routinely in literary criticism.

The External Evidence

It is well known that there are many references in the New Testament records to allegedly historical people (e.g., Pontius Pilate, Gallio, and Caesar Augustus); to places (e.g., Jericho, Egypt, and the Sea of Galilee); and to events (e.g. the Roman census, the crucifixion of Jesus, and a Palestinian drought). Indeed, Luke, traditional author of one of the Gospels and the Acts of the Apostles, consistently casts his writings in a historical context, for example: "In the fifteenth year of the reign of Tiberius Caesar–when Pontius Pilate was governor of Judea, Herod tetrarch of Galilee, his brother Philip tetrarch of Iturea and Traconitis, and Lysanias tetrarch of Abilene–during the high priesthood of Annas and Caiaphas..."[29] This is a real plus for our test purposes, as scholar F.F. Bruce points out: "A writer who thus relates his story to the wider context of world history is courting trouble if he is not careful; he affords his critical readers so many opportunities for testing his accuracy. Luke takes this risk and stands the test admirably."[30] What evidence led Bruce to that conclusion?

The Evidence of Archaeology

One of the most fruitful sources in this regard is the findings in the field of archaeology. Volumes have been written on specific details, mostly since the beginning of the twentieth century. Scientific archaeology is really only a little more than a century-and-a-half old. British scientists first pioneered the modern techniques that have led to a revolution of knowledge about ancient times. Perhaps it is safe to say that because of modern archaeology, more is known today about first century New Testament background than anyone has known about it since the third century. With so much data available today, it is no longer difficult to test the New Testament's claim to historicity.

James, son of Joseph, brother of Jesus

Hailed by *Time* magazine as the "most important discovery in the history of New Testament archaeology,"[31] a limestone bone box or ossuary that may once have contained the bones of James, the brother of Jesus, was discovered in 2002 in Jerusalem.[32] James is identified in

JAMES BONE BOX   BAS
Recently discovered first century burial box (ossuary) with the inscription: "James, son of Joseph, brother of Jesus" (*inset enhanced for clarity*).

the New Testament as one of the brothers of Jesus[33] and later as the leader of the Jerusalem church.[34] The reason this discovery made the front page of *The New York Times* and nearly every other newspaper in the world is that it bore an inscription in clear Aramaic letters: "James, son of Joseph, brother of Jesus." Archaeologists believe it is "the earliest archaeological attestation of three important figures– Jesus, James, and Joseph–in the history of Christianity."[35] James was martyred in A.D. 62.

Tests on the date of the limestone of the box, scientific examination of the patina of the inscription, and the writing style all support its authenticity and origin during the time period in which James died. Expert paleographers have confirmed the authenticity of the inscription. Hershell Shanks, editor of the professional journal *Biblical Archaeology Review*, has recently summarized the strong case of evidence for its authenticity.[36]

Is the "Jesus" on the box Jesus of Nazareth? A prominent statistician estimated that there is a 38% chance that only one individual in Israel at this time would have this combination of three names. There is only one other ossuary where a brother is identified, usually implying importance or fame. There are still skeptics and reasons to question the authenticity of this archaeological discovery.[37] If eventually proven to be the ossuary of James, the brother of Jesus, it would be an enormously important affirmation of the New Testament's historical truthfulness in its references to both Jesus and his family.

Pontius Pilate and Caiaphas

Pilate, identified in the New Testament Gospel accounts as the governor of Judea at the time of Christ's crucifixion, is confirmed by references to him in writings of the Jewish historian Josephus and the Roman historian Tacitus.[38] Additional confirmation came when archaeological excavation of the site of ancient Caesarea Maritima, the city from which he ruled, uncovered a two-by-three-foot cornerstone near the theater with the inscription: "Pontius Pilate, the Prefect of Judea, has dedicated to the people of Caesarea a temple in honor of Tiberius."[39]

Likewise, Matthew's Gospel mentions Caiaphas as the Jewish high priest who presided over the trial of Jesus.[40] In 1990, during road construction in Jerusalem, heavy equipment broke through the roof of a limestone cave or tomb used for burial in the first century. Located in the Peace Forest, the cave contained a sculptured bone box, or ossuary, with a name inscribed on the side. It was "Joseph Caiaphas," the same high priest mentioned by Matthew.[41] A tomb nearby likely belonging to the high priest Annas has also been found.[42]

These people and many others such as kings Herod the Great and Herod Agrippa II, emperors Augustus and Tiberius, and rulers Gallio and Sergius Paulus are part of the continuing discoveries of archaeology proving that the New Testament references are to real historical persons.

The Roman Census and Date of Jesus' Birth

"In those days Caesar Augustus issued a decree that a census should be taken of the entire Roman world. (This was the first census that took place while Quirinius was governor of Syria.)"[43] For many years the existence of a Roman census was questioned by critics of the New Testament. Papyrus census forms have been found dating from the first centuries B.C. and A.D., proving the practice was common during Jesus' lifetime and in His locality.[44]

Dr. Boyd Seevers

CAESAREA MARITIMA STONE OF PONTIUS PILATE
A building stone found in the city of Caesarea Maritima with an inscription that documents the historicity of both Pontius Pilate and Tiberius.

When it was discovered that the Roman Empire conducted its census only every fourteen years, critics said it didn't correspond to the year of Jesus' birth. Furthermore, the only time that anyone knew of a Quirinius being governor of Syria was A.D. 6. However, recent external evidence has again confirmed the historical accuracy of the New Testament.

We now know that King Herod the Great died in the spring of 4 B.C. and he was very much alive when Jesus was born. Based on this fact and that Jesus was "about thirty" when he began His ministry in A.D. 26, Jesus' birth must have been in the winter of 5-4 B.C.[45] How did we get it wrong? A sixth-century Roman monk dated the Nativity in the 753rd year from the founding of Rome, but his chronology was off by four to five years. Unfortunately his errant chronology was adopted in the Gregorian calendar, which is still used today.

What about the problem of Quirinius and the timing of the census? Archaeologist Sir William Ramsay found several inscriptions indicating that a Quirinius was indeed governor of Syria on two occasions. The first was several years previous to his appointment to that position by Augustus in A.D. 6. Evidence of a Quirinius has recently been found on an ancient coin that has him as proconsul of Syria and Cilicia from 11 B.C. until after 4 B.C.[46] He would have been the governor at Jesus' birth in 5 B.C. and the date of the biblical Roman census is now thought by many to have been conducted from 8 B.C. through 5 B.C., with the later time likely for an outlying area like Palestine. Again, this corresponds in time with the year of Jesus' birth. Even though the traditional year of Jesus' birth is certainly incorrect, His birth has nevertheless served as the anchor for the designations B.C. and A.D. for nearly everyone in the whole world for centuries.[47]

Jesus' Ministry

The existence of numerous specific cites which are referenced in the Gospels have been confirmed by archaeologists. The remains of a first-century house located under a fourth-century church in Capernaum is believed to be that of the apostle Peter, and where Jesus often stayed during his Galilean ministry. Archaeological excavations have found 131 inscriptions and monograms in the wall plaster there, including crosses

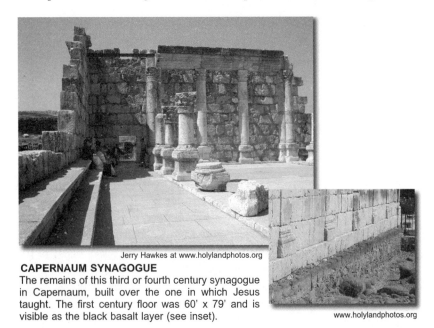

Jerry Hawkes at www.holylandphotos.org

CAPERNAUM SYNAGOGUE
The remains of this third or fourth century synagogue in Capernaum, built over the one in which Jesus taught. The first century floor was 60' x 79' and is visible as the black basalt layer (see inset).

www.holylandphotos.org

of different forms and the mention of Jesus as "Lord" and "Christ" in Aramaic, Greek, Syriac, and Latin. First century fish hooks, and graffiti references to "Peter" were also present.[48] A large octagonal Byzantine church was erected over this House of Peter in the fifth century. In 1990 the Franciscan church built a structure to protect and restore it.

Likewise in Capernaum, the 60x79-foot floor of a synagogue dating to the first century has been discovered (shown opposite).[49] This is the same synagogue which the New Testament says was built by a Roman centurion who loved the Jews, and where Jesus often preached during His ministry.[50]

In Jerusalem, excavations along the southern wall of the Temple Mount have uncovered a number of baptisteries used for ritual purification by immersion.[51] These are likely the ones referred to in Luke's Gospel which were used by Joseph and Mary before going on to the Temple Mount for Mary's purification after giving birth to Jesus.[52] Other external evidence uncovered by archaeologists relating to the historicity of Jesus' ministry includes the discovery of the pool of Bethesda in Jerusalem where Jesus healed the invalid;[53] the pool of Siloam at the end of the 1,749-foot-long tunnel of Hezekiah where Jesus restored the sight of a man who was born blind;[54] and the site of Gergesa (modern El Kursi) on the east side of the Sea of Galilee, where Jesus cast demons out of a man and into a herd of swine.[55] It is an amazing truth that we are able to go there today, two thousand years after Jesus lived, and still see the same places where He walked and ministered!

POOL OF SILOAM www.holylandphotos.org

South of the present walled city is the Pool of Siloam where Jesus sent a blind man to wash and receive his sight. Three flights of steps lead down into the pool (partially exposed on right).

Crucifixion of Jesus

The Gospel writers refer to the use of nails in the crucifixion of Jesus on a cross of wood. The accuracy of the reported use of nails, as opposed to tying the victim on the cross, and even the practice of crucifixion itself in Palestine, have both been questioned by critics. Surely, they said, the writers must have embellished their stories with unhistorical details. A recent publication suggests not.[56]

CRUCIFIXION VICTIM
Excavation in Jerusalem resulted in the discovery of the ankle and foot bones (and nail) of the only crucifixion victim ever found by archaeologists. The date was close to the time of Jesus' crucifixion. (The sketch above was based on a photograph.)
Figure 4.

I read with fascination a scientific article reporting on the only crucifixion victim ever discovered. The remains of a twenty-four- to twenty-eight-year-old man were found in a tomb near Jerusalem with a four-and-one-half- to five-inch-long nail through his foot.[57] His crucifixion was dated by the carbon-14 method at A.D. 42 (Jesus was crucified about A.D. 30) though Evans reports the date as the late A.D. 20s.[58] Once again, archaeology has confirmed the biblical account. They *did* have nails in Jerusalem at the time of Jesus, and they *did* use them for crucifixion–just like the Gospel writers reported!

Furthermore, the calf bones of this victim were "brutally fractured... clearly produced by a single, strong blow."[59] This was evidence supporting a Palestinian variation of the Roman practice of crucifixion, as referred to in the Gospel of John: "The soldiers therefore came and broke the legs of the first man who had been crucified with Jesus, and then those of the other. But when they came to Jesus and found that He was already dead, they did not break His legs."[60] The archaeologist explained:

> Normally, the Romans left the crucified person undisturbed to die slowly of sheer physical exhaustion leading to asphyxia. However, Jewish tradition required burial on the day of execution. Therefore, in Palestine the executioner would break the legs of the crucified person in order to hasten his death and thus permit burial before nightfall. This practice, described in the Gospels in reference to the two thieves... has now been archaeologically confirmed.[61]

Politarchs

During the apostle Paul's second missionary journey he visited the city of Thessalonica. Luke refers to the city officials there by the term "politarchs."[62] The problem was that this title had not been found in other ancient literature, and it was assumed by critics that Luke made up the term because he did not have firsthand knowledge of the area. They were quick to allege that this was an example of the New Testament's inaccurate history. Beginning with William Ramsay, classical scholar and archaeologist at Oxford in the late nineteenth century, at least thirty-two inscriptions containing this title have now been found by archaeologists. Nineteen come from Thessalonica; three of those are from the first century.[63] The most notable was Ramsay's discovery of Greek names under the phrase, "...in the time of the Politarchs" on a stone archway which stood at the entrance into the first-century city of Thessalonica, the same archway which the apostle Paul and Luke would have passed through.

Luke had it right—"politarchs" was the correct title of magistrates in some Macedonian towns. Though frequently questioned, Luke's historical accuracy has been vindicated by archaeological evidence. Indeed, F.F. Bruce says that Luke's "sure familiarity with the proper titles of all the notable persons who are mentioned in his pages" is "one of the most remarkable tokens of his accuracy."[64] He cites several pages of examples. After a lifetime of research, archaeologist William Ramsay acknowledged that the evidence changed his mind from one of skepticism and unbelief to the view "that Luke's history is unsurpassed in respect of its trustworthiness." He identified Luke as "a historian of the first rank," placing him "along with the very greatest of historians."[65]

Archaeological discoveries today are no longer relevant just for a few scientists or the curious adventurer. With the expansion of excavation in Israel and the advent of worldwide communication means like the Internet, people in homes and offices everywhere are becoming aware of the scientific facts which confirm the historical truthfulness of Jesus' life and the beginning of Christianity.

The Testimony of Scholars

The professional judgments of international experts also support the historical accuracy of the New Testament. William Albright, famous archaeologist of Johns Hopkins University, wrote:

The excessive skepticism shown toward the Bible by important schools of the eighteenth and nineteenth centuries, certain phases of which still appear periodically, has been pro-

"A young man who wishes to remain a sound Atheist cannot be too careful of his reading. There are traps everywhere— 'Bibles laid open, millions of surprises,' as Herbert says, 'fine nets and stratagems.' God is, if I might say it, very unscrupulous."
C.S. Lewis, Surprised by Joy

gressively discredited. Discovery after discovery has established the accuracy of innumerable details, and has brought increased recognition to the value of the Bible as a source of history.[66]

This theme is repeated again and again. For example, Millar Burrows of Yale stated that "archaeological work has unquestionably strengthened confidence in the reliability of the scriptural record. More than one archaeologist has found his respect for the Bible increased by the experience of excavation in Palestine."[67] This is a real challenge for those who demand evidence. To determine the truthfulness of New Testament statements, Dr. Burrows invites them to grab a spade and join him in checking it out! Nelson Glueck, renowned Jewish archaeologist, claimed that "no archaeological discovery has ever controverted a biblical reference."[68]

Finally, Kenyon, considered a foremost authority in this field, expressed what some have thought was an overly optimistic statement: "Archaeology has not yet said its last word, but the results already achieved confirm what faith would suggest, that the Bible can do nothing but gain from an increase in knowledge."[69] While this was written in 1948, Kitchen more recently affirmed that the "continuing discoveries and work of the intervening decades have not changed, merely enhanced, the truth of his [Kenyon's] judgment."[70] So much for my previously-described, uninformed view that Christianity and faith were anti-intellectual.

The Internal Evidence

Somewhere in my early years I picked up the view that the stories written about Jesus were really legends that had developed long after He was gone. During my college skepticism, I thought it was naive to believe two-thousand-year-old accounts if they were not written by those who lived at the same time as Jesus, and by those who knew Him personally. I couldn't imagine a better source than someone who was actually there.

Eyewitness Authors

Partly at that time, and extensively later, I discovered that this is exactly what the New Testament writers claim for themselves, i.e., that they were eyewitnesses or had eyewitness sources. Furthermore, the Gospel accounts of the words and deeds of Jesus were being proclaimed verbally within fifty days, and had limited circulation in written form within twenty-five years after His death and resurrection. The apostle Peter was able to stand in Jerusalem less than two months after Jesus' death, with those hostile to the Christian movement present, and say, "Men of Israel, listen to these words: 'Jesus the Nazarene, a man attested to you by God with miracles and wonders and signs which God performed through Him in your midst, just as you yourselves know....'" He went on to say that "this Jesus God raised up again, to which we are all witnesses,"[71] and there is no indication of any attempts to rebut these appeals to historic fact. Indeed, no one has yet been able to document such a rebuttal.

Imagine the difficulties today of trying to publish a totally fabricated biography of former U.S. president John F. Kennedy. In this fictitious account JFK is depicted as walking on water, healing the sick in front of crowds, raising the dead, and feeding five thousand people with five barley loaves and two fish. Following his death he was said to be resurrected and then to have ascended to heaven before over 500 eyewitnesses. As a result, a massive religious movement has begun in which JFK is worshipped.

> *"Faith is not blind... In the case of Christian faith it arose for the earliest disciples from historical contemporaneity with Jesus. They were not compelled by the evidence: plenty of people saw it and declined to commit themselves. But the evidence was the ground on which they committed themselves."* Michael Green, *The Truth of God Incarnate*

The only way this "biography" could be accepted by the public is if the book never fell into the hands of anyone who knew Mr. Kennedy, or if all who ever knew him were dead, and if other written accounts of his life and death had been destroyed. Otherwise, those who knew him would testify that it was untrue, as would the written evidence. If there were still a few hardy "believers" in JFK, his body could be exhumed which would put an end to all such nonsense.

Likewise, if there were any fabrication or departure from the facts about Jesus on Peter's part, it would be inconceivable that three thousand individuals would respond in repentance and faith to a person they knew to be a fraud or product of Peter's imagination.[72] This is especially true when we realize that to make such a confession would mean tremendous sacrifice, perhaps the loss of their businesses, their family and even their lives. If Peter knew his statements about Jesus were false, surely he was smart enough to leave Jerusalem and go where people had no firsthand knowledge of Jesus. But Christian teaching about Jesus' life, death and resurrection originated and was accepted in Jerusalem, where the people were in the best position to know whether or not it was true, and where accepting it could cost them dearly.

The apostle Paul, too, with his life on the line before the Roman procurator Festus and King Agrippa, appealed to the events of Jesus' life as historically true. He said, "The king knows about these matters, and I speak to him also with confidence, since I am persuaded that none of these things escaped his notice; for this has not been done in a corner."[73]

Early Date of Writing

Therefore, the extensive evidence which establishes the authorship of the New Testament documents within twenty to thirty years after Jesus' death makes the theory of legends untenable. As Bruce says, "The disciples could not afford to risk inaccuracies (not to speak of willful manipulation of the facts) which would at once be exposed by those who would be only too glad to do so."[74] No legend is known to have developed and become generally accepted within the same generation as the events and persons themselves.[75] Sherwin-White, Oxford historian of Roman times, explains why: "...[F]or these stories to be legends, the rate of legendary accumulation would have to be 'unbelievable'; more generations are needed... [E]ven the span of two generations is too short to allow legendary tendencies to wipe out the hard core of historical fact."[76]

Legal Proceedings

The legal proceedings against Jesus and Paul mentioned in the trial narratives of the New Testament correspond with what we know of Roman practice during that period of the first century A.D.[77] F.F. Bruce extends the accuracy even "to the more general sphere of local colour and atmosphere. He [Luke] gets the atmosphere right every time."[78] Such subtle inclusions in the New Testament writings could only be the result of authors who were actually there, i.e., who were eyewitnesses to the events they recorded.

A HIGHLY PROBABLE VERDICT

Based on the very methods which literary and historical scholars use today, the only reasonable and logical conclusion I can draw is that the Bible is the most reliable book of antiquity. If anyone chooses to reject the New Testament evidence as insufficient, honesty to the facts requires that they also reject all other ancient literature as well, whose evidence is quite inferior to that supporting the New Testament. For me, only my remaining prejudices caused me to stubbornly cling to my former skeptical views. Had I only known then the more complete evidence I have since learned and have included in this chapter, I do not believe my search would have been as prolonged.

> *"Prejudices are rarely overcome by argument; not being founded in reason they cannot be destroyed by logic."*
> Tryon Edwards, *The New Dictionary of Thoughts*

In the eighteenth century, the French skeptic Voltaire vowed that in one hundred years from his time Christianity would be swept from existence and passed into history. Instead, a mere twenty-five years after his death, the British and Foreign Bible Society was formed and issued over 229 million Bibles in its first one-hundred years of publishing. In fact, Voltaire's own printing press was later used to print copies of the Bible, and the Geneva Bible Society used his home to stack Bibles for distribution.[79] The reliable history on which the Christian faith is based makes it difficult to remove from an informed society. A.N. Sherwin-White, internationally recognized scholar from Oxford, has written that "for [the book of] Acts the confirmation of historicity is overwhelming... any attempt to reject its basic historicity even in matters of detail must now appear absurd. Roman historians have long taken it for granted."[80] He argues similarly for the Gospels. Indeed, Luke makes reference to thirty-two countries, fifty-four cities, and nine islands–without a single mistake.[81]

C.S. Lewis, professor of Medieval and Renaissance Literature at Cambridge University, acknowledged that the evidence for the historicity of the Gospels was a major factor in his conversion from atheism.[82] Frank Morison, an English journalist, set out to prove that the story of Christ was encumbered with legend and myth. He found by his research that the biblical records were historically valid.[83] Scores of others, right up to the present day, have searched the historical evidence and found it exceedingly convincing and compelling.

– FOCUS & DISCUSSION –

1. Why is it so important for the argument of God's existence that the New Testament is a trustworthy first-century historical record?

2. What evidence in this chapter, if any, was unexpected or came as a surprise to you? How did it change your opinion or understanding of the New Testament?

3. Based on the information in this chapter, how has the science of archaeology supported the historical reliability of the New Testament?

4. How well-known in society today is the evidence for the integrity and historical reliability of the New Testament as presented in this chapter? ...in the Christian community? Why do you think this is so?

5. What evidence weakens the allegation that the New Testament accounts of Jesus are only legends?

6. Suppose you were a participant in an event which occurred twenty-five to thirty years ago. Can you remember the incident sufficiently to detect a major fabrication of the event if it were presented to you verbally or in print? What implications does this have to the allegation that the Gospel accounts are fabricated legends, not historically true?

– Discoveries –

The material in Chapter 2 can be summarized in two additional "Ah-ha!" discoveries:

3. The New Testament records in our Bible today are essentially unchanged from eyewitness accounts of Jesus!

4. Archaeological discoveries have confirmed that the New Testament writings are historically reliable!

What's Next?

We have examined some of the evidence supporting the first and crucial condition for testing the claim that Jesus is God; that is, the need for a trustworthy first-century historical record concerning Jesus. The reader is now in the position to be the judge on this matter.

We must next turn our focus on what these historically reliable documents report about what Jesus of Nazareth said and did. To determine whether He was more than a man will require that we examine these primary sources for the data concerning His life. The jury, as far as that matter is concerned, is still out.

CHAPTER 3

IS JESUS REALLY GOD?
Looking At the Eyewitness Evidence

The Archbishop of Canterbury: "Jesus is the Son of God, you know."
Jane Fonda: "Maybe He is for you, but He's not for me."
Archbishop: "Well, either He is or He isn't."
Conversation on the Dick Cavett Show
(in *The Quest for Faith*, C. Stephen Evans)

When a person stops believing in God, he does not believe in nothing.
He will believe in anything.
G.K. Chesterton, British writer

J esus faced a most difficult task. He was born into a Jewish family two thousand years ago. He grew up in the small town of Nazareth in Israel, a remote and unimportant province of the Roman Empire. By every known indication He grew up as a normal boy who "kept increasing in wisdom and stature, and in favor with God and men."[1] However, when He was about thirty years of age He stood up in the synagogue of His home town and announced, in effect, "There is something I've been meaning to tell you–I'm God!"

If one of my friends or colleagues were to make such a statement, I would either laugh or cry. I would assume he was joking or had lost his mind! What makes Jesus' statement any different? The only way I could seriously consider such a claim is if He were to provide some powerful evidence to back it up. I would need some reasons that prove the guy's credibility.

That is where we are in our test as well. We found in Chapter 2 that we have every reason to trust the Gospel accounts of Jesus' life as reliable sources of history. Therefore, we can use them to test the Christian claim that Jesus is God.

What I am proposing is familiar territory to me. In my professional expertise in the field of ecology, I would occasionally take my students into the field to give them firsthand experience with the lecture subject. That's what I am going to suggest we do with the claim that Jesus is God—take a field trip. We can test the credibility of this claim for ourselves by stepping into the eyewitness' shoes via their accounts, and with their ears hear what Jesus claimed and with their eyes see what Jesus did.

TESTING THE CLAIM THAT GOD BECAME A MAN

Evidence of Jesus' Claims

Messiah[2]

The words I used for Jesus' announcement to His hometown are not actually a quote from the New Testament. Indeed, it could be argued that on that occasion He did not claim deity at all. The incident as recorded in the physician Luke's account indicates that Jesus read from the Old Testament book of the prophet Isaiah.[3] This was a very familiar prophecy which the Jews maintained would be fulfilled by their Messiah, or Christ, when He came. Jesus concluded His reading with the words, "Today this Scripture has been fulfilled in your hearing." In other words, Jesus said, "Here I am, ready or not!" Jesus was claiming to be the long-ago prophesied Messiah.[4]

This is a strong claim, and one He made on other occasions as well.[5] The response of the people who heard Him that day makes it clear how strong His claim was: they doubted Him. They asked, "Is not this Joseph's son?" Their questioning prompted Jesus to anticipate what would be a reasonable expectation under the circumstances when He said, "No doubt you will quote this proverb to Me, 'Physician, heal yourself...'" This was equivalent to our modern expression, "Prove it." It is clear from the context that the people rejected, temporarily at least, Jesus' claim to be the Messiah. Who is right? Only additional evidence can answer this question.

Lord God

Whether or not Jesus was the Messiah paled, however, compared to the issue raised in an encounter Jesus had with the Pharisees. In it He challenged their teaching that the Messiah was to have only a human nature. Matthew records His reasoning:

> Now while the Pharisees were gathered together, Jesus asked them a question, saying, "What do you think about the Christ, whose son is He?" They said to Him, "The son of David." He said to them, "Then how does David in the Spirit call Him 'Lord,' saying, 'The Lord said to My Lord'... If David then calls Him 'Lord,' how is He his son?" And no one was able to answer Him a word...[6]

The point of the question is that if David in the Old Testament Psalm refers to the Messiah as Lord, then the Messiah must be more than David's physical descendant. The phrase David used is "*Yahweh* [The Lord] said to *Adonai* [My Lord]." Both may be names of God and in English could be translated, "God said to God." David applies the second one to his descendant, the Messiah. Jesus was showing them how inappropriate it would be for David to refer to any other human by the divine title of "Lord." As scholar Tasker states, "In other words, the Messiah, though of Davidic descent, is also of divine origin."[7] Why would Jesus bring this up except to correct an oversight in their teaching concerning the Messiah's nature? Clearly He wanted them to understand that as their Messiah He was both man and God.

I AM[8]

Why was Jesus so subtle? Did He ever come right out and say He was God? In fact, that did happen on an occasion when the Jewish leadership asked Him point blank, "Whom do You make Yourself out to be?" Among other things Jesus replied, "Your father Abraham rejoiced to see my day; and he saw it and was glad." When we realize that Abraham lived about two thousand years before Jesus, we can understand their question, "You are not yet fifty years old, and have You seen Abraham?" Jesus then responded, "Truly, truly, I say to you, before Abraham was born, I AM." Jesus is claiming preexistence; that is, He lived before Abraham. Being born a baby in Bethlehem was not His beginning. Indeed, the way He phrased His answer in the present tense suggests that He had no beginning at all.

More importantly, Jesus applied the title "I AM" to Himself. This is one of the names of God from the Old Testament given to Moses at the burning bush incident.[9] For a man to do this was unprecedented. The Jewish contemporaries of Jesus were reluctant to even say the holy name of God for fear that their unclean lips might defile it. But Jesus not only put it on His lips; figuratively, if He had one, He would put it on His name tag as well.

The context of the passage further supports this view. Upon hearing His answer, they attempted to stone Jesus to death. This is clear evidence that they understood Him to be claiming deity, since only such a claim would be considered blasphemous and thereby warrant death according to their law—which is why they attempted to stone Him.

One with the Father[10]

Jesus was asked to clear up His identity on other occasions as well. At the winter Feast of Dedication in Jerusalem, He was asked again, "How long will You keep us in suspense? If you are the Christ, tell us plainly." Jesus responded, "I and the Father are one." What could He mean by that?

One possibility is that the Father and Jesus are "one and the same." This would mean that while Jesus was on earth, there was no one in heaven tending the universe. They would be the same person. The grammar of the Greek is helpful here. "One" would need to be in the masculine gender if this was the intended meaning. It is not. It's in the neuter gender.

The neuter gender could mean to be "in agreement" or "in unity." This would be somewhat equivalent to my saying I was in the will of God. But the context of the passage is against this. If that's what Jesus meant, they could not have justified the death penalty, which they clearly sought by attempting again to stone Him. Being in unity or agreement with God is what they all should have wanted.

The contemporaries of Jesus, who spoke the same language and shared the same culture, were in the best position to know what He meant by "one." Their understanding is clear in their statement, "For a good work we do not stone You, but for blasphemy; and because You, being a man, make Yourself out to be God." "One" here means "essence," that is, Jesus and the Father are equals. Jesus shares all the divine attributes of the Father. This fits the grammar and the context perfectly, and explains the Pharisees' reaction.

From Above and Not of this World[11]

During the years of my search for answers, I recall thinking that Jesus was, for the most part, quite like any other man. For example, His conversation was wise but didn't seem to me indicative of a claim to deity. I questioned why anyone bothered to attribute deity to Him at all. In hindsight, I realize I took that position out of ignorance: I really was not acquainted enough with Jesus' teaching to know any better. Later, when I began to read the Gospel records, I realized that many of His statements could never appropriately be a part of any other person's conversation.

Try, for example, using some of Jesus' words as your own with a neighbor across the backyard fence, such as, "You are from below, I am from above..." Unless you live in an upstairs apartment, you would certainly have startled him. To add Jesus' further words, "You are of this world; I am not of this world," may send your neighbor running–to call 911! These are not the statements of an ordinary man. To claim to be from another world and to add, besides, that unless people believe you are God ("I AM") they will die in their sin and be separated from God forever is to invite scoffing and scorn–unless you can somehow credibly back up your claims.

Give Eternal Life to Anyone[12]

Imagine yourself sitting at a rest island in a busy shopping mall. You beckon several people to you and discretely ask if they would like to live forever. Caught off guard, they stare silently back at you. You assure them that if, after further reflection, eternal life should sound like a good idea, they may look you up and you will grant it to them. I doubt that you would be overwhelmed by the traffic jam at your front door.

This is exactly what Jesus said–that He could give eternal life to whomever He wished. To Martha and Mary, devastated by the death of their brother Lazarus, Jesus said, "I am the resurrection and the life; he who believes in Me shall live even if he dies, and everyone who lives and believes in Me shall never die." What makes the difference between His saying it, and your or my saying it? All the difference in the world! You and I can't deliver on such a promise. Jesus did–He raised Lazarus from the dead in front of many eyewitnesses.

All Authority in Heaven and on Earth[13]

Imagine going to a conference of world leaders including the president of the United States, and looking them all in the eye and saying, "All authority has been given to Me in heaven and on earth." This is

A SUMMARY OF SELECTED CLAIMS OF JESUS		
1.	**He is the Messiah (Christ)** The Messiah is also identified as "Mighty God" and "Everlasting Father" in Isaiah 9:6.	Luke 4:14-21; John 4:25-26
2.	**He is the Lord God** The Messiah is of Davidic descent and of divine origin.	Matthew 22:41-46
3.	**He is the I AM** He existed before Abraham and can rightly bear the name of God.	John 8:53-59
4.	**He is One with the Father** He is one in "essence" – He possesses all the divine attributes.	John 10:30-33
5.	**He is from above and not of this world** He is of heavenly origin.	John 8:23-24
6.	**He can give eternal life to anyone** He has the right to grant eternal life to His followers and the power to guarantee it.	John 5:21; 10:27-28
7.	**He has all authority in heaven and earth** He is the Son of God with absolute authority in every domain.	Matthew 28:18; John 19:7

Figure 1.

another of Jesus' "ordinary" human statements which understandably would have been an affront to the great Roman Empire of His day. I believe it is well within the mark to suggest that if some of what Jesus said were put into our mouths today, we would be prime candidates to be locked up or treated for psychological disorders–and rightly so. Indeed, Jesus did die for His claims. Throughout history people have been sentenced for what they do, i.e., for a crime committed. But Jesus was crucified for who He claimed to be. As they said to Pilate, "...He ought to die because He made Himself out to be the Son of God."[14]

There can be little doubt from our field trip thus far, that one of the reasons Christians today think Jesus is God is because those who were with Him two thousand years ago report that He claimed to be God. The data of His life recorded by the eyewitnesses is quite convincing. Albert Schweitzer, who himself believed that Jesus misunderstood His own nature, nevertheless acknowledged that the evidence for His claim to be

God was good. The concern of his M.D. dissertation at Strasbourg in France was how Jesus could be sane and still claim to be God.[15] Figure 1 summarizes the evidence of Jesus' claims.

Evidence of Jesus' Actions

Many have claimed to be God. Hindu holy men can even draw crowds with alleged magical powers. Invariably, however, their lives fall short of deity, they lose credibility with their followers, and the movement disappears. Jesus is the exception. The more time people spent with Him, the more certain they were that His claims were valid. This is where the idea of our field trip is particularly valuable. We can see Jesus through the eyes of those who walked with Him. Luke recorded the history of what Jesus did for approximately two years following the people's rejection of His claim in Nazareth. During those two years many changed their minds about Him. Their transformation from skepticism to acceptance is striking. What changed their minds?

The answer to that question is obvious to anyone who takes seriously the history in the biblical accounts of Jesus' life. The eyewitnesses reported the astounding things He did. Many of His contemporaries were persuaded by these events to believe in His divine nature, even though they were predisposed against such a conclusion. If we are willing, we can now look for ourselves at what they saw Him do. We will continue our field trip.

Authority to Forgive and Remove the Consequences of Sin[16]

Several of the events Luke recorded in his Gospel are intriguing. Following His announcement in Nazareth to be the Messiah, Jesus went to Capernaum on the northwest shoreline of the Sea of Galilee. There, in what was likely the apostle Peter's home, many of Israel's most capable religious leaders–Pharisees and lawyers–had gathered. Because the pressing crowd limited access to the site, some men carrying a paralyzed man on a stretcher presented him to Jesus through a hole they tore in the roof of the house. Jesus immediately responded to the paralyzed man, "Friend, your sins are forgiven you." The scribes and Pharisees found that offensive: "Who is this man who speaks blasphemies? Who can forgive sins, but God alone?" What caused them to take offense?

Imagine that while I was speaking to a group, an individual jumped up, rushed to the platform, and knocked me down with a hard blow. Promptly he had a change of heart, apologized profusely, and begged my forgiveness. If I granted it, would the rest of my audience likely accuse me of blasphemy–usurping the prerogative of God to forgive my attacker?

Dr. Boyd Seevers

PETER'S HOME
Just across the street from the Capernaum synagogue, this hexagonal foundation of a fifth century building was built over the still evident remains of the first century home of the apostle Peter.

Not only is that unlikely, rather they would likely commend me for my benevolence. Somehow, the circumstances in Jesus' situation must have been different than those in my imaginary scene. Let me try again.

Once again someone in my audience nearly knocks me out, and immediately apologizes for it. Before I can respond, someone else from my audience comes forward and says to the one who hit me, "I want you to know that I forgive you for hitting Don." Even in my dazed condition, I would certainly question what this third party has to do with it. The offense was against me and it is only right that I should be the one offering forgiveness. This third party neither is in a position to forgive nor had the right to do so. Now to the Pharisees and lawyers, Jesus was this third party. It is unlikely He had ever seen this man before. As far as we know, the man had done nothing to Jesus which required His forgiveness. Whatever sin the paralyzed man had in his life was ultimately an offense against God. Therefore, God should be doing the forgiving! Since the religious leaders had not understood or accepted that Jesus was God, they reasoned He was guilty of blasphemy in that He, a third party, was usurping the position and right which are reserved only for God.

Furthermore, they were undoubtedly thinking this was just idle talk. They didn't believe He had actually removed the man's sin. After all, it's rather difficult to demonstrate visibly that you have forgiven someone's sins. In this case, however, there was a way. Luke records Jesus' response to the challenge:

> "But, so that you may know that the Son of Man has authority on earth to forgive sins,"–He said to the paralytic–"I say to you, get up, and pick up your stretcher and go home." Immediately he got up before them, and picked up what he had been lying on, and went home glorifying God. They were all struck with astonishment... saying, "We have seen remarkable things today."[17]

To instantly heal a paralyzed man and send him home carrying his bed is in itself stunning. How did this prove that Jesus had taken away the man's sins? The erudite group present there seemed quite persuaded. The answer is found in understanding a certain conviction of the Jews of that day; that is, they saw a direct relationship between sin and consequent judgment in the form of pain, suffering, etc. In the form of an equation, they would say:

Presence of Sin ⇨ Leads to ⇨ Consequence of Sin

In other words, if I were climbing a stairs with a group of first-century Jewish peers, and hurt myself in a fall, they would gather around and ask me what sin I had committed recently! This mind-set is illustrated even by Jesus' disciples on another occasion when they asked Jesus whether the plight of a man born blind was caused by his parents' sin or his own.[18] Therefore, when the paralyzed man on the stretcher was brought to Jesus, the religious authorities saw his paralysis as a consequence of his sin. This afforded Jesus an opportunity to visibly demonstrate, to their satisfaction, the removal of the man's sin, i.e., by healing him. If the presence of sin caused the presence of paralysis, the removal of paralysis meant to them the removal of the sin that caused it.

Removal of the Consequence of Sin ⇨ Proves ⇨ Removal of the Sin that caused it

The Pharisees and lawyers responded, "We have seen remarkable things today." They were not referring to the miracle of healing, but rather that Jesus did what only God can do–take away a person's sin. While Jesus used such logic to satisfy their need for overt evidence of His divine power that day, He did not actually share their simplistic view of the relationship between sin and its consequences.[19]

Authority over Death

At the southern Galilean city of Nain, Jesus met a procession en route to taking a widow's only son to burial. Jesus' action is recorded by Luke.

> When the Lord saw her, He felt compassion for her, and said to her, "Do not weep." And He came up and touched the coffin; and the bearers came to a halt. And He said, "Young man, I say to you, arise!" The dead man sat up and began to speak. And Jesus gave him back to his mother. Fear gripped them all....[20]

> "Ultimately, the problem of the meaning of history revolves around the question: 'Who is man himself and what is his origin and final destination?' Outside the central biblical revelation of creation, the fall into sin and redemption through Jesus Christ, no real answer is to be found to this question..."
> Herman Dooyerweerd, Dutch professor of philosophy

Fear indeed. Had I been present when the young man sat up in his coffin, I would have needed a place to sit down! Jesus had compassion for the widow, and raised her son from the dead. Many others present that day had compassion, too, but all they could do was weep. The gulf between the two is immense. The only way this incident would not revolutionize every reader's view of Jesus is if they denied it had ever happened.

On what basis would they do this? These are the most reliable records of antiquity. The people who saw this miracle that day realized Jesus was special, as indicated by their comments that "A great prophet has arisen among us!" and "God has visited His people!" Joseph's boy never did things like *this* before. It was getting harder and harder for His contemporaries to refer to Him as only the carpenter's son. In the first chapter we realized that death is the ultimate victor of our life if the finite triangle (the physical world) is all there is. Here, we see Jesus demonstrating that for those who trust in Him–the infinite and incarnate God–death doesn't win any more.

Authority over Nature[21]

Jesus and His disciples were crossing the Sea of Galilee in a fishing boat typical of the day, equipped with sleeping and storage space under

Jerry Hawkes at www.holylandphotos.org

JESUS BOAT
Buried in the sand of the Sea of Galilee, this twenty-seven-foot fishing boat discovered in 1986, dates to the time of Jesus and was undoubtedly similar (inset model) to those used by fishermen like Peter.

www.holylandphotos.org

a deck covering, when a severe wind, familiar to Galilean fishermen even today, threatened their lives. In the midst of His disciples' panic, Jesus was awakened. He "rebuked the wind and the surging waves, and they stopped, and it became calm." As a scientist I am acquainted with the laws of nature. In Jesus we come face to face with the law-Maker. His mastery over natural elements was so instant and decisive, that those who were with Him appropriately asked, "Who then is this, that He commands even the winds and the water, and they obey Him?" That is a very good question.

The incidents above are only four of the thirty-four miraculous events which the eyewitnesses of Jesus recorded in the Gospels. Could Jesus, were He a human teacher only, forgive sin against God, heal the physical body, raise the dead, and command nature to obey Him? Perhaps, some say, He was only like the prophet Elijah who, as a human, also did miraculous acts. But there was a significant difference between the two which would have been very evident, especially to the Jews of His day. It was characteristic of all the prophets to preface or conclude all they did with a "Thus says the Lord" or "Thus the Lord did." No prophet ever claimed the power to do a miracle apart from God.

Jesus, on the other hand, said, "I am the Resurrection and the Life," "I give eternal life," and "I am the light of the world." If He were only a prophet, then He would have been a blasphemer and a liar.[22]

Many Other Convincing Proofs

It was Jesus' strategy to give reasons for people to believe His claim to be God. His invitation was clear: "Do not believe Me unless I do what My Father does. But if I do it, even though you do not believe Me, believe the miracles..."[23] That is what we have been looking at, i.e., the miracles of Jesus. In addition, as a result of recent study, I have noticed other indications of Jesus' deity in the historical records as well.

Acceptance of Worship[24]

Before Jesus began His public ministry, He experienced forty days of temptation in the wilderness. When He was invited to worship the devil in exchange for an earthly kingdom, Jesus quoted the Law, "You shall worship the Lord your God and serve Him only."[25] Later, during His ministry, His followers directed their worship toward Him, and He accepted it without any indication of protest. In fact, He approved of it. One has to conclude that Jesus was either a disgusting hypocrite or saw Himself as worthy to receive that which was reserved for God alone. On another occasion Jesus was receiving praise, and justified it by quoting an Old Testament Psalm stating that God had prepared such praise for Himself.[26]

Authority over Demonic Spirit Beings[27]

At the city of Capernaum Jesus was confronted by a demon-possessed man. Jesus rebuked the demons, "Be quiet and come out of him!" There was uncontested obedience. Who would have such authority? There are not many choices. The Jewish religious leaders realized this and on one occasion accused Jesus of being demonic Himself, thereby casting out demons by Beelzebul, the ruler of the demons. The other choice is that He has authority because He is God. The response of the people who witnessed the Capernaum exorcism was, "What is this message?" or in other words, what does this demonstrate to us about who He is? They recognized that such authority was evidence He was more than a mere man.

Claim to be Sinless, the Only Way, and a Ransom for Mankind

The profile of Jesus which emerges from this sort of field trip into the historical records is often surprising to those who are skeptical. It was to me years ago when I doubted the truthfulness of the biblical accounts. While several of the observations I have included above are the result of more recent research, the limited knowledge I had at the time forced me to rethink my position about Jesus. In addition to all the rest, Jesus made several statements which, if true, make Him unique. He claimed to be without sin: "Can any of you prove Me guilty of sin?"[28] He said clearly that He is the exclusive way to God: "I am the way, and the truth, and the life; no one comes to the Father, but through Me."[29] And He stated that His life had such value as to redeem humankind to God, something no other human could do.[30] In view of all this, it is not surprising that Jesus caused such a revolution in the lives of His disciples.

A SUMMARY OF SELECTED ACTIONS OF JESUS		
1.	**He demonstrated authority to forgive sin** He forgave offenses that only God could forgive, and removed sin's temporal and eternal consequences.	Luke 5:17-26
2.	**He demonstrated power to raise the dead** He broke the bondage in which death held all people.	Luke 7:11-16
3.	**He demonstrated control over nature** He commanded and natural law obeyed.	Luke 8:22-25
4.	**He accepted worship from His followers** He accepted worship which He said was to be reserved for God alone (Luke 4:8).	Matthew 14:33; 28:17
5.	**He demonstrated mastery of demonic spirits** He commanded and the spirit world obeyed.	Luke 4:33-36
6.	**He lived a sinless life** No one was able to accuse Him of sin.	John 8:46
7.	**His life was uniquely valuable before God** He offered his life as a ransom to God for our forgiveness.	John 14:6 & Mark 10:45, with Psalm 49:7-9

Figure 2.

IDENTIFYING THE LOGICAL OPTIONS

It is inevitable that anyone acquainted with the historical data concerning Jesus will have to face up to a decision concerning Him. Jesus Himself raised the critical question to those who had witnessed this evidence in person for more than two years. At a retreat near Caesarea Philippi, at the base of Mount Hermon, Jesus asked the disciples, "Who do you say I am?"[31] Though removed in time two thousand years, the question is still extremely relevant. What would you say? What options do we have?

Jesus is a LEGEND

This view was popularized prior to the twentieth century and took on unmerited legitimacy only because the evidence which now refutes it was yet unknown. The position was reasonable when it was thought that the New Testament records were late second-century writings. With their early dating in the first century, within the lifetime of the eyewitnesses (as discussed in Chapter 2) this view is no longer tenable.

Jesus is a LIAR

Jesus claimed to be God and those who heard Him understood what He was saying. A logical examination of this claim could lead to three additional options concerning Him. First, either *He is* or *He is not* who He claims to be. Surveys continue to indicate that more than 90 percent of the people in this country believe there is a God or higher power. But if they were asked if Jesus is that God exclusively, many would be reluctant to go that far. It is common to hold the opinion that Jesus is only a wonderful man, a great moral teacher. Is this position logical in view of His claim to be God?

If Jesus claimed to be God and He is not who He claimed to be, then either *He knew it* or *He didn't know it.* Now if He claimed to be God, knowing that He wasn't, then He would be a LIAR. He would have lied about Himself, and received worship as if He were God Almighty. If Jesus is a liar, then He has deceived more people than any other human, for the Christian movement He began is the largest religion in the world. He could not be the greatest liar who ever lived, *and also* be a great moral teacher. Besides, He would be a fool, because He died for that lie.

Was Jesus a liar? No, because His character throughout the historical accounts support a person of virtue and integrity. No, because it is inconceivable that Jesus could sustain a committed following for several years without being detected as a fraud. No, because He was authenticated to be who He claimed to be by His resurrection from the dead.

Jesus is a LUNATIC

At first glance, the other option may seem more plausible, i.e., *He didn't know* He wasn't God. Jesus claimed to be God, was not, but really thought He was. Could Jesus have been deluded? O. Quentin Hyder, practicing psychiatrist in New York City, analyzed the records of Jesus' behavior, personality and relationships for symptoms of psychiatric disorders. He concluded his study by pointing out that the evidence does not support the view that Jesus was a lunatic. Rather, He demonstrated qualities of excellent mental health.

> A person is free to maintain that Jesus, out of honest delusion, made His claim to deity. But if one takes this position, he does so without any psychological evidence in its support and, indeed, in spite of considerable evidence to the contrary.[32]

Jesus is the LORD

Only one option remains. Jesus claimed to be God–and He is. He is the LORD. One final consideration carries a lot of weight to make this the option best supported by the evidence.

Jesus Claimed to be God

Figure 3.

THE CRITICAL EVIDENCE: JESUS' RESURRECTION

Jesus promised several times during His three-and-one-half year ministry that He would rise from the dead.[33] Indeed, when asked by the Jews what evidence He would give to authenticate Himself, He said, "Destroy this temple, and in three days I will raise it up."[34] He was, in fact, speaking of His own body, i.e., His own physical resurrection. This would be the central test to determine whether He was authentic. It should be noted that *all* other founders of world religions, e.g., Buddha and Muhammad, died. People go to their grave sites to pay their respects. Christians don't do that, however, because Jesus is not in a grave–He's alive. No other religious figure known to man has ever provided convincing objective evidence that he had risen from the dead. I don't believe it is possible to imagine any greater credential to authenticate Jesus' claim to be deity than His resurrection.

Did it really happen? Lord Darling, former Chief Justice of England and obviously trained to sift through the evidence, was satisfied that the resurrection was reasonably supported:

> The crux of the problem of whether Jesus was, or was not, what He proclaimed Himself to be, must surely depend upon the truth or otherwise of the resurrection. On that greatest point we are not merely asked to have faith. In its favour as a living truth there exists such overwhelming evidence, positive and negative, factual and circumstantial, that no intelligent jury in the world could fail to bring in a verdict that the resurrection story is true.[35]

What is this evidence which has persuaded people for centuries from all walks of life, even those who have skills honed to detect truth from error? There are three major arguments.

The Tomb of Jesus Was Empty

Even the disciples themselves were skeptical. They described the women's testimony that they had seen the resurrected Jesus as "nonsense."[36] After all, there was likely a sixteen-member Roman guard and a one-quarter- to one-ton stone with a Roman seal covering the entrance to the tomb. Disturbing it meant death at the hands of the guards or death to the guards who allowed it. Jesus' body was prepared for burial as a "mummy" with some seventy-five pounds of gummy spices inside strips of cloth.[37] The cloths were still in the tomb–but the body wasn't in them anymore.[38] Thomas said in effect that unless he saw the physical evidence of the nail prints in His hands, he would never believe it. Jesus showed them to him—and he believed.[39]

The Jewish authorities, who were in the best position to check out the facts, never attempted to refute the empty tomb, only tried to explain why it was empty.[40] Dr. Paul Maier, historian at Western Michigan University, sums up the current situation:

> Accordingly, if all the evidence is weighed carefully and fairly, it is indeed justifiable, according to the canons of historical research, to conclude that the tomb of Joseph of Arimathea, in which Jesus was buried, was actually empty on the morning of the first Easter. And no shred of evidence has yet been discovered in literary sources, epigraphy or archaeology that would disprove this statement.[41]

Jesus Appeared Physically to Many People After His Resurrection

The historical Gospels record ten distinct physical appearances by Jesus to people during the forty days after His death. He "appeared to Cephas [Peter], then to the twelve. After that He appeared to more than five hundred brethren at one time, most of whom remain until now, but some have fallen asleep..."[42] C.H. Dodd has commented, "There can hardly be any purpose in mentioning the fact that most of the five hundred are still alive, unless Paul is saying, in effect, 'the witnesses are there to be questioned.'"[43] These were not hallucinations because they were too diverse as to times, places and personalities. Besides, hallucinations are not collective to five hundred people, and the psychological condition of belief and expectation was lacking—the disciples were persuaded against their wills. Jesus' appearances were not mere illusions or fantasies. We know this because He stood with them and said, "See My hands and My feet, that it is I Myself; touch Me and see, for a spirit does not have flesh and bones as you see that I have."[44] He also ate with them.[45]

Moreover, the testimony from negative sources is especially convincing. Jesus appeared to His brother James, who had rejected Him during His public ministry. James later became the leader of the Jerusalem church which proclaimed the resurrection.[46] The apostle Paul testified that it was the appearance of the resurrected Jesus to him when he was Saul of Tarsus—an enemy and persecutor of believers—which converted him.[47]

> Make no mistake: if He rose at all it was His body; if the cells' dissolution did not reverse, the molecules reknit, the amino acids rekindle, the Church will fall . . .
>
> John Updike, *Seven Stanzas at Easter*

The Lives of the Disciples Were Transformed

It is a well-known fact that the disciples of Jesus abandoned and denied association with Him during His arrest, trial and crucifixion.[48] The reason was fear for their own lives. Subsequently, the disciples had real experiences that they believed were literal appearances of the risen Jesus. They were transformed from scared men hiding in the Upper Room into bold proclaimers of His resurrection. They were even willing to die for their conviction. Indeed, all but one of the eleven remaining apostles died a martyr's death, yet none ever denied seeing Jesus alive after His death, not even to save their very lives. People will die for what they believe to be true, but none will die for what they know to be false. Gary Habermas, apologist and philosopher, a specialist on Christ's resurrection, has drawn an important conclusion: "The disciples' transformation shows that they really believed that Jesus rose from the dead and disproves the fraud (stolen body) theory both because of this change and because liars do not make martyrs."[49] The Watergate political scandal in the United States during the mid-70s illustrates this point. Sophisticated lawyers, faced with the threat of a few years in prison, were unable and unwilling to maintain their fraudulent cover-up.

J.N.D. Anderson, former director of the Institute of Advanced Legal Studies at the University of London, rightly said that the resurrection is "either the supreme fact in history or it is a gigantic hoax..." and if it is true, then "to fail to adjust one's life to its implications means irreparable loss."[50]

A HIGHLY PROBABLE VERDICT

The reader must be the judge of the evidence. Is it reasonable to consider Jesus as a liar, a lunatic, or merely a wonderful moral teacher? Oxford professor C.S. Lewis did not think so:

> I am trying here to prevent anyone saying the really foolish thing that people often say about Him: "I'm ready to accept

Jesus as a great moral teacher, but I don't accept His claim to be God." That is the one thing we must not say. A man who was merely a man and said the sort of things Jesus said would not be a great moral teacher. He would either be a lunatic–on a level with a man who says he is a poached egg–or else he would be the Devil of Hell. You must make your choice. Either this man was, and is, the Son of God; or else a madman or something worse. You can shut Him up for a fool, you can spit at Him and kill Him as a demon or you can fall at His feet and call Him Lord and God. But let us not come with any patronizing nonsense about His being a great human teacher. He has not left that open to us. He did not intend to.[51]

> *"But the intellectual case for Christianity became powerful to me after reading* **Mere Christianity** *[by C.S. Lewis]. At the end of the week I could not imagine how you could not believe in Jesus Christ."*
>
> Charles Colson, chairman of Prison Fellowship

Our imaginary field trip through the Gospel accounts, though far from exhaustive, did examine a broad sample of the available historical data. As much as anything from ancient times can be, I believe the evidence validates the claim that Jesus is the incarnation of the infinite, personal God. Dr. Edwin Yamauchi, eminent scholar and archaeologist, has testified that "the historical evidence has reinforced my commitment to Jesus Christ as the Son of God who loves us and died for us and was raised from the dead. It's that simple."[52]

The implications of this truth have the potential of significantly changing our view of life. The issues are more than academic, they are also moral. You are faced with the decision to accept or reject Him as Lord. You have the freedom to turn away. But the stakes are too high to take the matter lightly. Jesus said,

> "I am the resurrection and the life; he who believes in Me will live even if he dies, and everyone who lives and believes in Me will never die. Do you believe this?"[53]

– Focus & Discussion –

1. Why is it so significant to Christianity whether or not Jesus is God? Do you agree that whether Jesus actually is God is the most significant issue of Christianity's validity? Why or why not?

2. Eyewitnesses to Jesus reported that He had authority over demons, death, sickness, and nature, and that He could forgive and remove the eternal consequence of sin. Why are these statements important for determining His identity?

3. Based on the evidence of Jesus' actions presented in this chapter, can you think of other options which could be attributed to Jesus other than the three listed (liar, lunatic, or Lord)? If so, explain and discuss.

4. What changed the minds of Jesus' contemporaries, even of many skeptics, from unbelief to faith that Jesus is God? (See Thomas: John 20:24-28; Saul: Acts 9:1-20.) Discuss the role of evidence and reason as a basis for faith in Jesus.

5. How did the information in this chapter impact your own understanding of who Jesus is?

— DISCOVERIES —

Two more *"Ah-ha!"* discoveries summarize the evidence we have considered in Chapter 3:

5. Eyewitnesses testified that Jesus claimed to be God!

6. The compelling evidence of Jesus' miracles and resurrection from the dead confirmed His claim to be God!

Ah-ha!

Discovery #6
Jesus Backed His Claim

Discovery #5
Jesus Claimed to be God

Discovery #4
Historically Reliable Records

Discovery #3
Eyewitness Records

Discovery #2
God Became Flesh

Discovery #1
No God? DEATH Wins

WHAT'S NEXT?

The historical evidence we have considered in this chapter supports the Christian claim that Jesus is the incarnation of the infinite and personal God of the universe. Consequently, each of us is faced with the need for a personal response to Him.

Of course, this choice leads us to the question of "faith." How do you get faith? Can faith be reasonable? Is faith just wishful thinking or can it be a certainty? When is faith valid? These are the important questions we will explore in the next chapter.

CHAPTER 4

CAN FAITH BE REASONABLE?

The Central Principles of Faith
The Life-Changing Dimensions of Faith

*"My biggest problem had always been the intellectual reservations.
I knew there was a God, but I could never see how man could
have a personal relationship with Him."*
Charles Colson, former special counsel
to President Richard Nixon

*"What we do with what we know
is what Christian knowing is all about."*
Os Guinness, author

Recently I was talking with a woman whose conviction and desire
was to follow Jesus. I will never forget her reason for hesitation. It
had little to do with the intellectual concerns of purpose in life,
the historical reliability of the Bible, or the deity of Jesus. On those issues
she had been satisfied. Instead, her hesitation was really a fear: "Will it
make me into a sap?"

CONTEMPORARY STEREOTYPES OF FAITH

The misunderstandings of religious faith run deep in our society. A
middle school teacher asked one of the young students, "What do you
think faith is?" Without even a pause, the answer was given, "That's

believing what you know isn't true!" When a university student was asked the same question, he said that "faith is believing what you cannot know."

That is not an uncommon idea of faith—as though faith is a second- or third-best way of operating in life. Knowledge, by which is meant intellectual apprehension, is assumed to be the best way. If one cannot know, then the next best thing is just to believe anyway. The implication being that such a position is at best precarious, if not actually being stupid (a "sap").

Sometimes religious people earn labels such as "anti-intellectual" or "those weak enough to need a crutch." A religious group in Arkansas made national news when their alleged faith got them into trouble with the law. Claiming to have received a vision from Jesus Christ that He was returning to the earth very soon, in faith they quit their jobs, kept their children home from school, and waited. Eventually they lost their homes because they could not pay the mortgages. Social welfare officials placed their children in foster homes and back into schools. The parents presented a caricature of faith on the evening news in homes across America.

More recently, national news focused on a court case where parents were being tried for the death of their daughter. Of what crime were they allegedly guilty? They claimed to have "faith" that God was going to heal their daughter. Therefore, they refused any medical care for her. She died.

Can faith be reasonable? Most negative impressions of faith are generated in us by what we see in other people, such as the much-publicized sexual abuse scandals by clerics in the church. Such impressions may also be generated by the eccentric neighbor next door, a devoutly religious yet strange aunt, etc. Interestingly, none of these stereotypes is derived from a careful study of the Bible itself. We don't want a concept of faith derived from someone's bad example. Rather, we should seek to know the meaning of faith straight from the source. Therefore, we will study the Bible to identify the principles and components of faith. Only then can we know whether faith is intended to be reasonable.

THE CENTRAL PRINCIPLES OF FAITH

Sometimes there is confusion about the word "faith." Recently I asked some people to identify differences that may exist between the words "faith" and "believe." Several explained distinctions with considerable confidence. The fact is that in the Bible, "faith" is the noun and "believe" is the verb form of the same Greek word. They are interchangeable as illustrated in the familiar John 3:16: "For God so loved the world that He gave His one and only Son, that whoever believes [has faith] in Him shall not perish but have eternal life." There is no difference in meaning if the words in brackets are used in place of "believes."

1. Faith always has an object

This first principle of faith is fairly obvious. When someone tells me they believe, my response is always to ask, "In what?" They never answer, "In nothing." Everyone recognizes that to believe or have faith is "in something" rather than "in nothing." We believe that the bungee cord won't snap, our car will get us home, or that the roof of the building is constructed so it won't collapse. In other words, we don't have faith in faith, but rather in the *object* of our faith.

2. Faith is only valid if its object is certain

The second principle is critical to understanding why the Christian faith is unique. Faith is not the same as sincerity, nor do feelings make faith genuine. Suppose I were asked if I believed a certain chair could hold me. Since other people were sitting on similar chairs, and since I am no heavier than they, and since the chair looked perfectly normal, I could be confident that it would hold me. Being impatient with further questioning on the matter, I exclaim emphatically, "I have no doubt in my mind the chair will hold me!" However, if someone slipped in earlier and cut the legs through so that the least touch would topple it, my confidence and sincerity would be of no avail. My faith is only as good as the object in which I place it. If the chair is good, my faith will be good. If the chair is bad, no matter how devout a believer I am, I am destined for a fall and my faith is betrayed.

A tragic incident at a local hospital was reported in the media. A nurse connected a patient to an "oxygen" source, and he immediately died. The source was mislabeled. It was actually a poisonous gas. Was the nurse competent and sincere? Did she really believe the gas was oxygen? Yes, on every count. She was also sincerely wrong. The object of her faith was defective, thus her faith was in vain.

We have already discovered that the object of Christian faith is the person of Jesus. If the facts about Him are not true and He is not who He claims to be–that is, the incarnate Son of God–then no amount of sincerity, confidence, or religious experience can make my faith in Him valid. This is precisely the conclusion of the apostle Paul to the people at Corinth: "But if there is no resurrection of the dead, not even Christ has been raised; and if Christ has not been raised, then our preaching is vain, your faith also is vain... your faith is worthless; you are still in your sins."[1]

I frequently ask Christians if their faith can save them. Their immediate response is usually, "Yes." They are initially offended when I tell them that no religious faith can save anyone. They are relieved though when I add, "But, the object of your faith, the all-powerful and redeeming Lord JESUS CHRIST, CAN!" Our *faith* is not the Savior; Jesus is. Likewise, can a person's faith provide life after death? Again, religious faith cannot secure life after death. The *object* of Christian faith, the One who conquered death, the Lord JESUS CHRIST, CAN!

The critical faith principle I came to understand is that the object of one's faith saves and secures life after death, not faith itself. Therefore, the validity of faith and religion is not determined by trying to generate more sincere or confident feelings, by emotional ecstasy, or the extent of personal sacrifice. Rather, a religion's validity is dependent on the genuineness and certainty of its faith object. Your faith is only as good as its object!

This is why Christians must be careful how they determine what truth is. For example, which of the two options below is correct?

- Jesus Christ is God because I believe it (have faith in Him)

- I believe Jesus Christ is God (have faith in Him) because it is true

Your answer, whether the first or second option above, will have important implications for comparative religions. If your choice is the first one, then you must admit that the millions of other "gods" in the world are also true. There are millions of Muslims who confess, "Allah is God because I believe it (have faith in him)." Likewise, there are millions of Hindus who say, "Brahman is God because I believe it (have faith in him)."

How can Christian faith be different from the faith of Muslims and Hindus? The central point of distinction between religions is the object they are trusting for their life and eternity. The historical evidence in Chapter 2 demonstrating that Jesus is the genuine article–the Son of God–sets Him apart from all other "god" claims. He is the only One who demonstrated in His ministry that He can remove the sin which separates us from God; and is the only One who demonstrated in history His power over death. That's why He claimed to be the only way to the Father.[2] This means that "there is salvation in no one else; for there is no other name under heaven that has been given among men, by which we must be saved."[3]

The second answer above is better: "I believe Jesus Christ is God (have faith in Him) because it is true." The Christian mission, therefore, is not about claiming superior and more devout faith and judging the sincerity, morality, or culture of other religions; but instead merely informing and inviting people to transfer their trust (faith) to a true and certain object–Jesus Christ. After all, that's what Jesus Himself said we should be doing: "...telling people about me everywhere..."[4] and proclaiming "...repentance for forgiveness of sins... in His name to all the nations..."[5]

THE BIBLICAL COMPONENTS OF FAITH

The Essential Components

1. Knowledge

A close synonym which may be substituted for the word faith is "trust." The university student who said that "faith is believing what you cannot know," would have quite a different impression if "trust" were substituted for "faith." Let me illustrate. "Do you trust so-and-so?" I ask, naming a person with whom the student is not familiar. He would likely respond, "How can I trust him since I don't even know him!" "But," I would remind the student, "You said that 'faith (trust) is believing what you cannot know.' Now you say that you cannot trust (have faith) in someone if you do not know them. Which is correct?"

The apostle Paul leaves little doubt which one he thinks is correct. Writing to the people at Rome, he communicates an interesting and logical sequence.[6]

We must **call** on the Lord to be saved	➤	To call we must **believe** in Him	➤	To believe we must **hear** about Him	➤	To hear we must have someone **tell** us	➤	To tell they must be **sent** out

Figure 1.

Paul says some go and tell so others can hear and believe. He then summarizes his teaching on faith: "Consequently, faith comes from hearing the message, and the message is heard through the word of Christ." The meaning of this has been paraphrased for clarity: "Belief, you see, can only come from hearing the message, and the message

> *"No intelligent person desires to substitute prudent acceptance of the demonstrable for faith; but when I am told that it is precisely its immunity from proof which secures the Christian proclamation from the charge of being mythological, I reply that immunity from proof can 'secure' nothing whatever except immunity from proof, and call nonsense by its proper name."*
>
> J.S. Bezzant, English theologian

is the Word of [concerning] Christ."[7] According to the apostle, faith cannot start without knowledge of its object. As stated earlier, I don't believe "in nothing"; I believe "in something." That "something" in the Christian faith comes from knowledge about the words, deeds, and person of Jesus.

This is why the Christian faith is evangelistic and mission driven. As Jesus said, "...you will be my witnesses, telling people about me everywhere..."[8] This is also why it is so critical for us to know whether the New Testament is an authentic and historically reliable source concerning Him. Without eyewitness testimony it would not be objectively possible to determine whether Jesus was credible in His claims and convincingly backed them up with His actions—thereby demonstrating Himself to be a worthy and valid object of faith.

The apostle Paul is right. I can only put my faith in Jesus if I know about Him. And only if that knowledge is supported by historical evidence of His deity can I be confident that my faith in Him is valid. I cannot even get started into the area of personal faith without using my mind and interacting with the evidence. This first component of faith as taught in the Bible is certainly more attractive than the anti-intellectual caricature of faith I had as a college student.

2. Will

The famous tightrope walker, Blondin, crossed the 1,100 foot expanse of Niagara Falls, 160 feet above the raging waters, at least twenty-one different times. On one occasion he accomplished the amazing feat blindfolded, and on another while pushing a wheelbarrow, to the amazement of thousands of onlookers. Promoters of these events asked the public for volunteers who *believed* he could do it again–and would be *willing* to prove their conviction by allowing Blondin to carry them across on his back. Although most professed to *believe* he would successfully cross the gorge, none were *willing* to risk the crossing with him. Finally, his agent and manager agreed to trust his life into Blondin's care. He was safely delivered to the other side, clinging to the aerialist's shoulders.

Knowledge is one thing, but choosing to commit one's life to that knowledge is another matter. Likewise, knowledge of Jesus is indispensable to faith, but it is only the first component. I could know exhaustively the evidence supporting the life of Jesus, and have no faith at all. The second faith component involves our will. This is illustrated once again in Paul's letter to the people at Rome.

> But not all the Israelites accepted the good news. For Isaiah says, "Lord, who has believed our message?"...But I ask: Did they not hear? Of course they did... Again I ask, Did Israel not understand?... But concerning Israel He [God] says, "All day long I have held out My hands to a disobedient and obstinate people."[9]

The people of Israel had disobeyed God, i.e., they lacked faith to trust Him. Paul is questioning why that was so. He asks the question whether they knew what God wanted. If not, the reason for their lack of faith would be a lack of knowledge.

I had a similar experience with my sons. Upon leaving my home for the day, I gave instructions for them to mow the lawn. When I returned that evening I noted that either the grass had grown at an unprecedented rate in the last few hours or they had failed to do what I had asked. I strongly suspected the latter. I went to them and used a question familiar to every parent, "Didn't you hear me?" Did I really think that the physics of sound waves had failed at the very moment I spoke my instructions to them that morning? No, I was quite confident my voice had reached their ears, but I was giving them the benefit of the doubt with my question. It turned out they did not have a knowledge problem. They had a "will" problem–they didn't *want* to mow the lawn.

In the passage above, Paul uses the same approach. He also concludes that the Israelites' problem was not caused by a lack of knowledge, but due to disobedience and obstinacy, i.e., a "will" problem.

Several years ago my wife and I had a disagreement. I no longer remember the issue, but it occurred on a Sunday afternoon. As I recall it (?!) she was wrong, and I was right, but she wouldn't admit it! About the time we were getting quite intense with each other, the doorbell rang. Answering the door, I was greeted by some good friends from another city who had stopped by because they were in the area. The transformation which immediately took place in my wife and me would make metamorphosis from a worm to a butterfly pale in comparison! We were instantly congenial and pleasant. After our friends left, I reflected on what had happened. What was it that changed us? The doorbell?

I was not that naive. The doorbell did not change us—we did. By a deliberate choice, an act of my will, I changed. Why didn't I change sooner? I certainly knew from seminars, books, and experience that my obstinate behavior was inappropriate to maintain harmony in a marriage relationship. The reason I didn't change before the doorbell rang, though, was that I didn't want to! I was exercising my will.

Faith is like that. In spite of the knowledge concerning Jesus which we have gained, if we do not exercise our wills, we have all the faith we are ever going to have: none. Unless we make a choice concerning who Jesus is, there will be no faith. A consenting will is the second essential component of the Bible's definition of faith. That is certainly more attractive than the caricature of faith as mere emotion which I had rejected years earlier.

3. Response

Faith is knowing the truth about Jesus, and being willing to accept Him. But one of Jesus' parables identifies another factor in faith: Faith is not the same as good intentions.

"What do you think? There was a man who had two sons. He went to the first and said, 'Son, go and work today in the vineyard.' 'I will not,' he answered, but later he changed his mind and went. Then the father went to the other son and said the same thing. He answered, 'I will, sir,' but he did not go. Which of the two did what his father wanted?" "The first," they answered. Jesus said to them, "I tell you the truth, the tax collectors and the prostitutes are entering the kingdom of God ahead of you. For John came to you to show you the way of righteousness, and you did not believe him, but the tax collectors and the prostitutes did. And even after you saw this, you did not repent and believe him."[10]

The point Jesus makes is that faith is proven by its action. If there is no response derived from the will and the knowledge, then there is no faith either. In other words, according to the teaching of the Bible, to qualify as legitimate, faith must consist of all three components: knowledge, will, *and* response. Frequently, I talk with people who consider abandoning any further pursuit of truth, once they are satisfied intellectually and are no longer inclined negatively toward it. They want to walk away at that point without making any response. But response is concerned with the implications of the truth for my life. James, the brother of Jesus, is quite concerned with this third component of faith when he says that "faith by itself, if it is not accompanied by action, is dead."[11]

The three corners of a triangle (see Figure 2) can be used to represent the three essential components of biblical faith. Based on this diagram, faith is "traveling the triangle." Jesus spoke a parable illustrating that there are really only two types of people; that is, those who travel the triangle and those who don't. The consequences in their lives are amazingly different:

> And why do you call Me, "Lord, Lord," and do not do what I say? Everyone who comes to Me, and *hears* My words, and *acts* upon them, I will show you whom he is like: he is like a man building a house, who dug deep and laid a foundation upon the rock; and when a flood arose, the river burst against that house and could not shake it, because it had been well built. But the one who *has heard*, and *has not acted accordingly*, is like a man who built a house upon the ground without any foundation; and the river burst against it and immediately it collapsed, and the ruin of that house was great. [*Emphasis added.*][12]

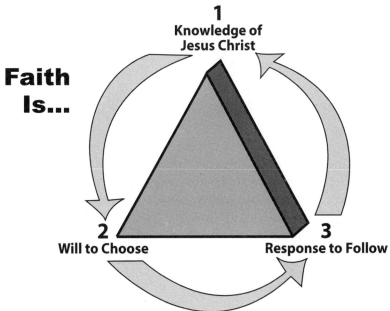

Figure 2.

The story is told of a fisherman with an enviable reputation–he always caught a large quantity of fish. But he also always fished alone. An elderly gentleman from a distant city, saying he wanted to learn fishing as a retirement hobby, begged the fisherman to teach him the sport. He refused repeatedly but the persistent doggedness of the retiree finally broke him down. At the lake the elderly man was surprised that the great fisherman had only a metal box and a net for gear. Upon reaching a remote corner of the lake and leaving the motor running, the fisherman opened his metal box, pulled out some dynamite sticks, lit them, heaved them overboard and raced the other way in the boat. After the blast, he circled around and began netting the fish which had been stunned. The senior citizen had seen enough of this fishing method. He pulled his game warden badge from his pocket and flashed it before the fisherman. With but a momentary pause, the fisherman pulled out more dynamite, lit and thrust it into the game warden's hand with the comment, "Now, are you going to fish or are you just going to sit there!"

Faith is like that. I have heard people say that they wish they had someone else's faith. Often they have exactly the amount of faith they are willing to have. They have not even responded to the knowledge they already have about Jesus.

The Resulting Definitions

It is usually helpful to attempt a definition of a subject to enhance communication. Rarely, however, have I encountered a definition of faith. Faith is easier to illustrate than define, but I have created two definitions which have helped me.

Head to Foot Commitment

The first is a homely one derived from a brief anatomy lesson. (I always assume that every one's favorite subject in school was biology!) If we were asked to parallel the appropriate anatomical parts with the three points of the faith triangle, our likely choices would be the head as knowledge, the heart as will, and the feet as response. Consequently, we may define faith as "making a commitment to God from head to foot." At least it is simple! Had I heard such a definition when I was questioning everything in college, I would either have denied its truth, or I would have had to rethink my caricatures.

I would never have imagined faith starting with the head, i.e., with reason, evidence, and knowledge. This definition says that once the mind is satisfied, the process, figuratively speaking, moves to the heart where the will must interact with the data concerning Jesus. I imagined that people of faith were "no-minds" who acted on the basis of emotion or need alone. Finally, the definition, again figuratively, moves the process to the feet or the place where there is life response. The whole person is satisfied, and a new alignment or orientation to Jesus is established.

> *"Hell is God's great compliment to the reality of human freedom and the dignity of human choice."*
> G.K. Chesterton, British writer

A Commitment-Making Process

The second definition is more descriptive: Faith is a commitment-making process, based upon the Word of God, and without regard to any emotional questioning of that Word.

A Commitment-Making Process...

I find it helpful to apply the definition to starting a new business—let's say a fast-food restaurant. I would want to begin with some market research on the eating preferences of people in the area, the number of competing businesses already operating, the availability of a building site, etc. The gathering of this critical information is equivalent to the "knowledge" component of the faith triangle. Yet I do not have a restaurant even if I have the most complete market research ever done. Eventually my interaction with the information must result in a choice whether or not to build. Even if my choice is affirmative, I still do not have a business. The knowledge and choice must be followed up with building, contracting with suppliers, hiring, and a variety of other responses consistent with the former two components. The commitment-making process I have just described is analogous to traveling the faith triangle. I study the person of Jesus, make a confession of faith concerning Him, and then follow Him in obedience.

...Based upon the Word of God...

However, the definition does not stop there. It has two conditions to guide the commitment-making process. First, the source is to be the Word of God which we have analyzed for reliability in Chapter 2. It may also include evidence about Jesus as discussed in Chapter 3. Finally, in the sense that the Word of God is seen as the truth of God, we may even include evidence in the natural world such as order and design. This is certainly superior to the ignorance, prejudice, and deception which had shaped my earlier beliefs.

...Without Regard to any Emotional Questioning of that Word.

The second condition recognizes human emotion as a reality, but denies that it should determine the outcome of the commitment-making process of faith. Emotions are not always consistent with what is right—jealousy, lust, depression, and insecurity being obvious examples. Furthermore, a faith commitment to follow Jesus may run counter to emotions which are linked to peer pressure, popularity, and pride. Therefore, it is better to recognize that emotions add an in-depth, whole-person experience, but within the context defined by the Bible's teaching.

The Premier Example: Abraham

An incident in the life of the Old Testament patriarch Abraham will help to illustrate this definition of faith. Isaac was a miracle child for Abraham and Sarah. Born when they were very old, he was a child through whom God promised to give them descendents as numerous "as the stars of the heavens" and "as the sand which is on the sea shore," and through whom "all the nations of the earth shall be blessed."[13] Isaac, born so late in his parents' lives, their only child, and the subject of such marvelous promises, was very dear to Abraham and Sarah.

Then the day came when God tested Abraham's faith: "Take now your son, your only son, whom you love, Isaac, and go to the land of Moriah; and offer him there as a burnt offering on one of the mountains of which I will tell you."[14] The thought is repulsive, but this event prefigured another one which would be the single most important event in the history of humankind.

I could think of a lot of reasons to sleep late the next morning after hearing a message like that. But Abraham rose early to go—I suppose because he felt so good about it! No, but he chose (will) to be obedient (response) to the Word of God he had received (knowledge). The emotional questioning that undoubtedly flooded through him did not determine his response. But struggle he did. How could God fulfill the many promises that He made concerning Isaac if Isaac were dead? He knew God is righteous and can not be unfaithful. By the time he arrived at the place of sacrifice three days later, he had resolved it in his mind: "Abraham reasoned that God could raise the dead..."[15]

As they walked up the mountain, Isaac asked an extremely pertinent question, "...where is the lamb for the burnt offering?" Obviously he didn't know yet! Abraham, the loving father, must have stammered and gulped hard. He then spoke prophetically, "God Himself will provide the lamb for the burnt offering, my son." But, temporarily, it was Isaac who ended up on the altar. Not until Abraham raised the knife to slay his son did God cry out, "Do not lay a hand on the boy... Now I know that you fear God, because you have not withheld from Me your son, your only son." I'm sure Abraham did not debate with God whether He was certain that He wanted to change His mind about Isaac! With great rejoicing that his son could live, he accepted a substitute sacrifice which God had indeed provided–a ram caught by its horns in a thicket. God did provide the lamb for the sacrifice, just as Abraham had told Isaac. Abraham was so grateful that he worshiped God using the name, Jehovah-Jireh, which in Hebrew means "The Lord Who Provides." This all took place on a mount called Moriah, which in Hebrew means "The Place of Provision." Put together it is "The Lord Who Provides in This Place."

It is natural to focus on the intense human elements of this event, while knowing nothing of its greater significance. Most would think the event has no relevance for our lives today, but that is a serious oversight. The "land of Moriah" where this event took place about 2000 B.C., is now known to be the area of Judea around Jerusalem. In actual fact, it is the hill or mount on which the Jewish temple was later built which was known as Mount Moriah.[16] It is the same hill that Abraham two thousand years earlier had referred to as "The Place of Provision," and where the Jews in Jesus' day sacrificed many lambs as the atonement for their

TEMPLE MOUNT IN JERUSALEM
Dr. Carl Rasmussen at www.holylandphotos.org
The Temple Mount in Jerusalem (left of center, surrounded by wall) is identified with the ancient Mount Moriah in the incident with Abraham and Isaac recorded in Genesis.

sin, according to Mosaic Law. When Jesus first began His public ministry, He was introduced by John the Baptist as "the Lamb of God, who
takes away the sin of the world!"[17] At the temple, God offered His only
Son Jesus to die so that many children of Abraham could live, i.e., "to
those who are of the faith of Abraham." The lamb which God provided to spare Abraham's son physically, foreshadowed the Lamb (Jesus)
which God provided two thousand years later *on the same hillside* so that
Abraham's descendents by faith could live spiritually and eternally. The
Lord truly did provide for us in that place.

> Consider Abraham: "He believed God, and it was credited to him
> as righteousness." Understand, then, that those who believe are
> children of Abraham. The Scripture foresaw that God would jus-
> tify the Gentiles by faith, and announced the Gospel in advance to
> Abraham: "All nations will be blessed through you." So those who
> have faith are blessed along with Abraham, the man of faith.[18]

> Therefore, the promise comes... by grace... for us who believe in
> Him who raised Jesus our Lord from the dead. He was delivered
> over to death for our sins and was raised to life for our justification.[19]

It is hard to imagine that this is all just coincidence. The "seed" [singu-
lar] of Abraham, i.e., Jesus Christ, has made possible spiritual descendents
of Abraham all over the world who number as the stars and sand grains, a
blessing to every nation on the earth, including the Gentiles (non-Jews).
If we trust Jesus as our Savior and Lord, then we are among those descendents of Abraham through our faith–"stars" and "sand grains" which God
promised to Abraham about four thousand years ago.

THE LIFE-CHANGING DIMENSIONS OF FAITH

Even if I had known about the biblical principles, the three components, and the definitions of faith during my search for answers as
a young man, I don't think I would have responded to them. It would
have helped remove some of the vagueness of the concept in my mind.
But there was still a big question about faith which bothered me a lot:
I wasn't sure I would be able to keep it up. At that time, I viewed being
a Christian as following a set of behavioral rules and regulations. I de-
spised hypocrites, and I certainly didn't want to be one. Later I realized

that my concern stemmed from a critical misunderstanding of how a person becomes a Christian.

A New Relationship: The GIFT of God's Presence

I viewed faith as a human enterprise–choosing a set of spiritual guidelines to follow. The focus was on how well I might be able to match my life to the rules. The day came when I discovered that faith is a relationship–with God. Since that time my study and experience have confirmed this truth. The discussion that follows is the way I would explain the life-changing dimensions of faith today.

Jesus, at the autumn Feast of Tabernacles in Jerusalem, focused attention on this matter:

> On the last and greatest day of the Feast, Jesus stood and said in a loud voice, "If anyone is thirsty, let him come to Me and drink. Whoever believes in Me, as the Scripture has said, streams of living water will flow from within him." By this He meant the Spirit whom those who believed in Him were later to receive.[20]

It is obvious that Jesus was referring to something supernatural–the Spirit of God within a person. How could this be? The naturalistic presuppositions of my scientific training had caused me to view such an idea with incredulity. But there is no mistaking the teaching. The night before His crucifixion, Jesus told His disciples that after He ascended they would receive another Counselor, the Spirit of truth, who "will be in you."[21] The apostle Paul affirms this, too: "Do you not know that your body is a temple of the Holy Spirit, who is in you, whom you have received from God?"[22]

How and when does this happen? Paul explains in his letter to the believers at Ephesus: "And you also were included in Christ when you heard the word of truth, the Gospel of your salvation. Having believed, you were marked in Him with a seal, the promised Holy Spirit, who is a deposit guaranteeing our inheritance..."[23] The "seal" is a mark of authenticity–that the believer really is a member of the family of God. The "deposit" is an earnest or token of what is to come, signifying that God will never

> "It is not a mere acceptance of certain beliefs and dogmas, though they are necessary, but essentially it is living in close fellowship with Christ. It is not only a religion to be practiced, but also a life to be lived."
>
> Bishop John A. Subhan (convert from Islam)

abandon His followers in this life, and assures fulfillment of His promise to give them eternal life after death.

This adds a relational dimension to the faith triangle. When we travel the triangle, thereby trusting in Jesus Christ as the object of faith, we receive the divine person of the Holy Spirit to live within us. The teaching that the Christian faith is more than a moral code to live by is indispensable to one's understanding of its dynamic nature.

That is why Jesus was so direct when He spoke to Nicodemus, a representative of the very religious Pharisaic party.[24] Nicodemus lived by a high ethic; he was a moral man. But Jesus told him he was not going to heaven ("enter the kingdom") on that basis alone. Rather, he must be "born of the Spirit." Literally, the expression "born again" means to be given new life from above. Many people I talk to think they will go to heaven because they have cleaned up their act or have gone straight. They think it is something they can pull off if they try hard enough. This is not so. Jesus said we become Christians when God does a miracle of spiritual conception within us as we respond in faith to Him. The result is a faith in which we experience the gift of God's presence changing us within instead of one which controls us by an external code of dos and don'ts.

A New Freedom: The GIFT of God's Grace

So, as a young person, I had completely misunderstood the nature of the Christian faith. I now know it is not so much a religion as it is a relationship. Some reflection upon Jesus will help us to see why. Christians do not think of themselves as following the teachings of Jesus, but rather Jesus Himself. The reason is simple–Jesus is alive. You can find disciples of Muhammad or Gandhi but only in the sense that they try to live by the teachings these leaders left behind. Muhammad and Gandhi are dead. Their followers cannot have a personal relationship with them. In contrast, a Christian's faith is a relationship with the person of Jesus Christ who is very much alive, experienced by His gift of the Holy Spirit within, and whom he/she fully expects to see face to face.

This insight helps to erase a frequent misunderstanding, i.e., how to get and sustain faith. Some may understand me to be saying that faith is, first, exercising their will to affirm Jesus, and then, second, exerting a little discipline to order their lives according to His teachings. That is what people think who haven't looked seriously at what Jesus has to say. His example and teachings are relentless: "...love your enemies..."; "...every one who looks on a woman to lust for her has committed adultery with her already in his heart..."; "...no one of you can be My disciple who does not give up all his own possessions..."; forgive one another "seventy times seven" times; "...you are to be perfect..."!

After a few weeks or months of clenched fists and teeth gritted in sheer determination, a person will become exasperated trying on his or her own to conform to these standards. Bertrand Russell, British mathematician and philosopher, once said, "The Christian principle 'Love your enemies' is good,... except that it is too difficult for most of us..."[25] Trying to live like Jesus is not just difficult–it is impossible. Until we are shaken by the experience of our own moral ineptness, we will not appreciate the need for the gift of God's grace in our lives. We will also resist Jesus' analysis of our condition.

> He [Jesus] went on: "What comes out of a man is what makes him 'unclean.' For from within, out of men's hearts, come evil thoughts, sexual immorality, theft, murder, adultery, greed, malice, deceit, lewdness, envy, slander, arrogance and folly. All these evils come from inside and make a man 'unclean.'"[26]

In the privacy of our own hearts and minds, we all know what He said is true. As the British writer, G.K. Chesterton, said, the one doctrine of Christianity which is empirically verifiable is the fallenness of man.[27] Some may deny it, but our experience of trying to be really good only serves to remind us of the need for grace, i.e., unmerited favor. The apostle Paul explains: "For it is by grace you have been saved, through faith–and this not from yourselves, it is the gift of God–not by works, so that no one can boast."[28] Grace was necessary because we are morally inadequate before a holy God: "There is none righteous, not even one... no one who seeks God."[29] In fact, if you have an interest in God and are attracted to faith, it is not your own doing, for Jesus also said, "No one can come to Me unless the Father who sent Me draws him."[30] One biblical passage in particular sums all this up quite clearly:

> But when the kindness and love of God our Savior appeared, He saved us, not because of righteous things we had done, but because of His mercy. He saved us through the washing of rebirth and renewal by the Holy Spirit... so that, having been justified by His grace, we might become heirs having the hope of eternal life.[31]

In view of these life-changing dimensions, the three corners of the triangle (below) are no longer adequate to represent faith. The compo-

Figure 3.

nents are right, but as sinful humans we lack the desire and the power to do it. What if the Holy Spirit Himself is placed at the center to create a supernatural dimension? For us even to be open to the evidence concerning the Bible and Jesus requires the convicting activity of the Holy Spirit. Twentieth-century theologian J. Gresham Machen described the process. "What the Holy Spirit does in the new birth is not to make a man a Christian regardless of the evidence, but on the contrary to clear away the mists from his eyes and enable him to attend to the evidence."[32] If, by His prompting, we respond and accept the gift of salvation through faith in Jesus Christ, the Holy Spirit takes up permanent residency within us. He transforms our fallen nature and desires from within, and provides the power to travel the triangle. As Paul says, "... [I]t is God who works in you to will and to act according to His good purpose."[33]

A New Hope: The GIFT of God's Heaven

The Christian faith promises a new relationship with the God who is really there. It also promises a new freedom from having to be good enough to earn God's approval. His grace means forgiveness, and new power and joy in life. Yet one preconceived fallacy about faith still remains.

I grew up thinking that no one in this life could ever know whether or not God had approved of them. That was a judgment only God could make after I had died, and the good and bad deeds had been tallied. I had to try as hard as I could and hope for the best.

It should now be apparent that this notion is inconsistent with the biblical principles of faith. How can one's destiny be uncertain if the object of faith, Jesus Christ, is certain? How can our deeds be the deciding factor if our relationship with God is a matter of grace? The apostle John sets the record straight:

> God has given us eternal life, and this life is in His Son. He who has the Son has life; he who does not have the Son of God does not have life. I write these things to you who believe in the name of the Son of God so that you may *know* that you have eternal life.[34] [*Emphasis added.*]

It is clear that God has already revealed the basis on which we can know who will go to heaven. In one of the most familiar passages in the Bible, He said that "whoever believes in Him [Jesus] shall not perish but have eternal life."[35] The apostle Paul said that "the free gift of God is eternal life in Christ Jesus our Lord."[36] We can know right now that there is life after death, and that we will spend it eternally in heaven with God.

Testing Subjective Claims

Our testing of the claim that Jesus is God and the truth of the Christian faith began by looking only at the objective evidence of science and history. It is now obvious that there are also some very important subjective, experiential elements as well. Sometimes I am told that these subjective, anecdotal aspects don't really prove anything. Josh McDowell answers this challenge with an illustration.

> For example, let's say a student comes into the room and says, "Guys, I have a stewed tomato in my right tennis shoe. This tomato has changed my life. It has given me a peace and love and joy that I never experienced before..." It is hard to argue with a student like that if his life backs up what he says... A personal testimony is often a subjective argument for the reality of something.... There are two questions or tests I apply to a subjective experience. First, what is the objective reality for the subjective experience, and second, how many other people have had the same subjective experience from being related to the objective reality?[37]

When asked how he accounts for his life change, the student would answer, "A stewed tomato in my right tennis shoe." But to find even one other person in the entire world who has had a similar life change as a result of a stewed tomato in their right tennis shoe is improbable. The objective reality is more than a little suspect when it cannot be verified repeatedly by others.

When a Christian is asked for the objective reality which has resulted in a significant subjective life change, he/she would answer, "The person of Christ and His resurrection." How many others share this same result from a relationship with Jesus Christ? The evidence is overwhelming. There are millions of people from every nationality, race and profession who have experienced this kind of positive life change. Such broad confirmation greatly increases the validity of the subjective, life-changing dimensions of faith in Jesus.

Before Jesus left this earth He told His followers that He was going to prepare a place for them in heaven. He added: "And if I go and prepare a place for you, I will come back and take you to be with Me that you also may be where I am."[38] According to Jesus, the time is coming when every person who has ever lived will stand before Him as judge. There is only one issue raised on that day of accounting: What did you decide to do about Him?[39]

It will be too late on that day of judgement to change your side—the choice will already have been made in life. It is the better wisdom to deal with this issue before then—to settle out of court! Then you can have the assurance which the apostle Paul had: "Therefore, there is now no condemnation for those who are in Christ Jesus... [He] set me free from... sin and death."[40]

– FOCUS & DISCUSSION –

1. Having learned about the principles and components of faith, explain how a person's commitment to follow Christ can be considered reasonable (based on an informed choice).

2. The point was made in this chapter that the Christian faith is reasonable. Suppose that a friend said to you, "If I had reasons, I wouldn't need faith." How would you answer?

3. Does including the third component ("Response") in the definition of faith support the unbiblical teaching that good works are necessary so you can earn heaven? (See Ephesians 2:8-9.) Try to make a case for a "no" answer to this question.

4. Jesus taught that those who put their faith in Him would be given the presence of the Holy Spirit within them (John 7:37-39). Why is this necessary? Refer to the following Bible passages to assist in your response: Isaiah 59:2; John 8:34; Romans 3:22b-23; 5:12; 6:23a.

5. Do you think *becoming* a Christian is more of a reformation or a transformation? Which image is most appropriate to becoming a Christian: a) remodeling an old house (reformation); or b) metamorphosis of a caterpillar into a butterfly (transformation)?

6. Three life-changing dimensions of the Christian faith were identified in this chapter. Discuss how these life-changing dimensions about becoming a Christian are the same and different from your previous understanding. How do you respond to them: Excited? Skeptical? Accepting?

– DISCOVERIES –

Two more *"Ah-ha!"* discoveries summarize the evidence we have considered in Chapter 4.

7. Christian faith is valid because its object, Jesus Christ, is certain!

8. Becoming a Christian is a MIRACLE of new life by the Holy Spirit, resulting in a new relationship, new freedom, and new hope!

Ah-ha!

Discovery #8
New Relationship, Freedom, Hope

Discovery #7
Certain Object, Valid Faith

Discovery #6
Jesus Backed His Claim

Discovery #5
Jesus Claimed to be God

Discovery #4
Historically Reliable Records

Discovery #3
Eyewitness Records

Discovery #2
God Became Flesh

Discovery #1
No God? DEATH Wins

WHAT'S NEXT?

We have discovered that God does a miracle in our lives when we confess faith in Jesus. Grace and forgiveness are necessary because we are morally and spiritually bankrupt before a holy God. As a result of His provision for us, we can have a personal relationship with God because we are created anew by the Holy Spirit who indwells us. God Himself offers to transform our lives by inspiring our wills and empowering our response to obey His Word.

Now we want to reflect on our personal life. We want to step back and see our own doubts and faith in proper perspective. We need to know exactly where we stand in regard to unbelief, doubt, and faith. We wonder what the implications and meaning of the position we hold will be for our life. The next chapter will provide great insight to the important question, "Where am I?"

CHAPTER 5

WHERE AM I?
Analyzing Unbelief, Belief, and Doubt

*"I thought it was very peculiar that I had acquired everything I had
wanted as a child–wealth, fame and accomplishment in my career, I
had beautiful children and a lifestyle that seemed terrific, and yet I was
totally and miserably unhappy. I found it very frightening
that one could acquire all these things and still be so miserable."*
Racquel Welch, actress

❧

*"The probability of life originating from accident is comparable
to the probability of the unabridged dictionary resulting
from an explosion in a printing factory."*
Edwin Carlston, biologist at Princeton

Several years ago my wife and I were doing a community survey
of people's views concerning the Christian faith. A rather large,
robust man came to the door at one home. When I asked him,
"Would you be willing to answer some questions concerning faith?" he
nearly exploded. The tirade that followed, accompanied by his anger,
red face and bulging eyes, was frightening. Fortunately, my wife was
there and I managed to hide behind her through most of it! Not wanting
to leave on a sour note, we changed the subject to compliment him on
his manicured lawn, and beautiful flower beds. We hit a positive nerve.
Being a yardsman myself, we engaged in a lively exchange of ideas and
strategies. Before we left his home, I wanted to find out how to avoid a

repeat performance of this encounter at the next house we visited. Had we done something to cause his ire?

He told us his story. At a previous residence he had lived alone except for a very special pet dog. He also had what he called a religious neighbor. On one occasion he let his dog out in the morning and was watching through the window. About the time the little dog was doing to the neighbor's shrubbery what dogs do to shrubbery, the neighbor stepped out of the bushes where he had been hiding and kicked the little dog nearly to the street. (Undoubtedly there was the religious neighbor's side of the story–which I was not hearing.) Because of internal injuries, the little dog had to be put to sleep. By this time the man is again red in the face and blurted out, "Now if that is what faith is like, I don't want any part of it!"

My first estimate of this man was that he was clearly a resolute unbeliever. After hearing his story, I knew it was not that simple.

THE ANALYSIS OF UNBELIEF AND DOUBT

Could such unbelief as this man expressed be justified by the circumstances? Is this man's unbelief different from that of others who do not believe, but have no hostility at all? Where do the familiar spiritual doubts fit into the subject of faith? To have a more complete understanding of these matters, it is necessary to examine the counterparts of faith, namely unbelief and doubt. As a result, we will be able to determine more specifically in which position each of us stands.

The Nature of Unbelief

Over the years I have asked many groups of people to tell me what comes to their minds when they hear the word "unbelief." Typically, they produce many of the following one-word descriptions:

doubt	unsure	blind	rejection
unknowing	decision	wavering	rebellion
distrust	ignorance	indecision	arrogant
skepticism	willful	hard-hearted	

Even a casual examination of these words suggests that they do not represent a single concept. Indeed, there is quite a difference between "ignorance" and "rejection," and between "wavering" and "rebellion."

Are these diverse descriptions the result of my surveying confused people, or are they honest attempts to communicate a complex subject?

Imagine with me that a lost tribe has just been discovered in the jungles of the Amazon. I volunteer to go to them so I can share the historical facts concerning Jesus. Assuming language compatibility, our dialogue makes me acutely aware of the consequences of their years of isolation. They have never heard of any events from outside their civilization, much less the details about Jesus. They are in unbelief concerning Him; that is, they lack faith in Jesus. In this case there is a special reason for their unbelief: ignorance. Remember: "How can they believe in what they have never heard?" Knowledge is the first component necessary for faith. They do not know about Jesus, the object of Christian faith. Let's identify their condition as "ignorant unbelief."

Now imagine that I spend every day, for several months, tirelessly telling these people about the basis for purpose and meaning, the historical and scientific evidence for the biblical writings, and what Jesus said and did. After each session the people question and debate. Some are persuaded by a point or two, but wonder about others. They are back and forth over the issues, unable to establish a firm position concerning Jesus. They are still in unbelief, but for a different reason: they can't decide. Remember: The second component necessary for faith is an affirming will. They will need to make a choice about Jesus. Let us label their new condition as "doubt."

Finally, after an additional period of teaching and questioning, the chief stands up to render his decision. To my horror it is now revealed that they are a cannibal tribe—there is a lot at stake here! The chief suggests to the others that I am "out to lunch." They reject the message concerning Jesus. They are in unbelief, but for a third reason: they have *chosen* not to believe. Let us express this condition as "decisional unbelief."

The Forms of Unbelief

We are now able to make sense of the diverse list of one-word descriptions of unbelief which people usually give. They identify three aspects of the complex nature of unbelief which can be categorized into the conditions through which the lost tribe progressed.

1. IGNORANCE – unknowing, blind

2. DOUBT– distrust, skepticism, unsure, wavering, indecision

3. DECISION – willful, hard-hearted, rejection, rebellion, arrogant

Unbelief exists in these three forms. The many words which come to people's minds when they think of unbelief are just synonyms of the basic three forms. The relationship between the forms is clarified by the diagram in Figure 1.

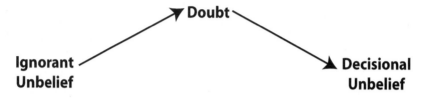

Figure 1.

The simplicity of determining the position we are in with regard to Jesus Christ should be apparent. I recall the time in my own life when I could no longer say I didn't know enough about Jesus–that I was ignorant of the facts. Interestingly, in my own mind, I had not decided to reject Him either. Or had I? My first exposure to the evidences for the Bible and for faith had left me unsure and wavering, i.e., in doubt. I went through a necessary time of discrimination and hesitation before a firm position could be taken. Additional months of fact gathering did not change my indecision. I had already been persuaded that the evidence for Jesus' deity was excellent. Yet I remained in doubt and kept thinking that I needed to read one more book, check out one more fact, and so on, *ad infinitum.* Looking back on this time from my perspective today, I believe my skepticism had become, in reality, decisional unbelief masquerading as doubt.

The Causes of Unbelief and Their Antidote

There are two primary blocks to a reasonable biblical faith. They are ignorance and willful rejection. The reason for this is evident when we recall the faith triangle. Knowledge concerning Jesus and an affirming will are the first two essential components of faith. When ignorance replaces knowledge and willful rejection replaces affirmation, there can be no faith.

If I were in ignorant unbelief, how could I get out of that condition? I would search for, be open to, and receive the readily-available information concerning the object of faith–Jesus. To illustrate this point, some years ago five Christian missionary couples were in South America attempting to tell the Auca Indian tribe about Jesus. The tribe was clearly in ignorant unbelief since the missionaries had not even met them yet, or understood their language. One day, while attempting to make personal contact, the five husbands were killed by the Aucas in a surprise attack. In spite of their tremendous grief over the loss of their husbands, the wives flew over the tribe and dropped gifts from their small airplane. This act of courage, love, and forgiveness eventually won them the opportunity for contact, and later, communication with the people.

Ignorance concerning Jesus was removed by teaching the facts about His life. The Aucas later made a faith commitment to accept Jesus as their Savior. An incredible life change took place. In fact, the chief of the tribe later baptized the son of the missionary he had personally killed.[1]

What if I were in the unbelief position of doubt concerning Jesus? How could I move from that position? I must decide how much information is enough to give relative certainty about Jesus' identity, and to say either "yes" or "no" to Him as my Savior and Lord.

> "Contemporary unbelief does not rest on science as it did towards the close of the last century. It denies both science and religion. It is no longer the skepticism of reason in the presence of miracle. It is a passionate unbelief."
> Albert Camus, French writer

Finally, what would I do to get out of my position of decisional unbelief? Since this is a position of choice or decision, there is no other way out than choosing to reconsider my position. Thereby I would be returning to the "doubt" position, where I again examine the evidence to see if a "yes" to Jesus is not more reasonable and appropriate than a "no."

However, sometimes it is not that clear-cut. The two causes of unbelief, that is, ignorance and unwillingness, may be interrelated. The apostle Paul, speaking of certain unbelieving people, wrote, "They are darkened in their understanding and separated from the life of God because of the ignorance that is in them due to the hardening of their hearts."[2] It is disconcerting to think that if we fail to respond positively to what we know is true, a hardening of the heart may take place which immunizes us, so to speak, against hearing and accepting additional truth. We have already indicated above that we are free to harden our hearts and willfully say "no" to the knowledge of Jesus we already have. That remains our choice. Yet we now are forced to accept that our hard-heartedness may make us blind to truth—unable even to recognize it—by our very refusal even to listen or be open to the evidence at all. Furthermore, our stubborn wills may even attempt to rationalize the rightness of such an untenable position.

Sometimes I have wondered about the irate man whom my wife and I had called upon at his home. What form of unbelief was he in? My first impression was decisional unbelief. He appeared to be rebellious and hard-hearted. After hearing his story, however, I changed my mind. I think he was in ignorant unbelief. He had rejected a caricature of faith, not the real thing. He seemed to know very little truth about Jesus at all. The concern I had for him was whether his anger over a foolish act by his so-called religious neighbor would forever shut him off from receiving the correct knowledge about Jesus which he would need to make a legitimate choice. Because of the stereotypes and caricatures of faith in society today, I have come to believe that ignorant unbelief, caused by a lack of familiarity with, or a refusal to listen to or be open to, the evidence, is the most common form of unbelief. In fact, this is the position from which the apostle Paul said he came as a former persecutor of Christians: "...yet I was shown mercy, because I acted ignorantly in unbelief...".[3]

THE ANALYSIS OF BELIEF

The observation that we have free will results in the possibility of our saying "no" to the truth claim of the Christian faith. But to be truly free means that we may also choose to say "yes." This is the alternative to one of the unbelief positions, i.e., belief. Figure 2 indicates the positions we may be in, and the choices we are free to make.

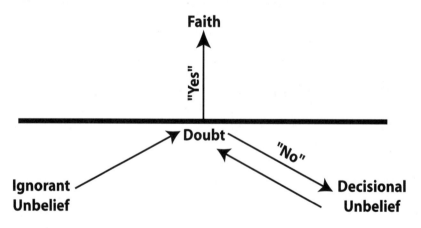

Figure 2.

The Operation of Belief

The idea that faith required a personal commitment became clear enough to me during my own search for certainty about God. What I did not understand at all, though, was the way in which faith was to operate in my life. Only later have I come to recognize that there is a counterfeit of faith which masquerades as the real thing. If the counterfeit is mistaken for the genuine, our faith in God can lead to disappointment and bitterness rather than fulfillment.

The Counterfeit: Contract Faith

There was a time in my life when I thought of faith in terms of a contract. The scenario went something like this: I was to believe that Jesus was the Son of God. In return, God would provide certain benefits for me–happiness, success, wealth, and health–small things! This seemed only right in view of the sacrifice it was for me to conform my life to following Him. And I would continue to follow God as long as He lived up to His end of my imaginary contract. If He didn't come through to meet my expectations–well, forget it! In other words, this scenario describes a faith contract with conditions written in language such as "I'll believe if ..."

A classic example of this approach to faith is seen in the life of Thomas, one of Jesus' disciples. Jesus had told His followers on several occasions that He would rise from the dead.[4] When Thomas was told by eyewitnesses that it had actually happened, he responded by saying, "Unless I see the nail marks in His hands and put my finger where the nails were, and put my hand into His side, I will not believe it."[5] One week later Thomas saw, and touched, then fell at Jesus' feet and exclaimed, "My Lord and my God!" Jesus then said to him: "Because you have seen Me you have believed; blessed are those who have not seen and yet have believed."

What was Thomas' problem? His alleged faith in Jesus was conditional–he insisted that he must physically see Jesus rather than believe the resurrection on the basis of what Jesus had promised beforehand. Thomas said, in effect, that he did not believe in Jesus because he would not trust His Word (nor the eyewitnesses) but would only believe if... and expressed his conditions.

In rescuing the nation of Israel from slavery in Egypt, God demonstrated His faithfulness by overcoming impossible odds with many miracles. He then brought them to the land of Canaan and promised that He would take them in. Twelve men were sent into the country as spies for forty days, and returned with two reports.[6] The majority report of ten said that while the land was excellent, the inhabitants were giants and their cities strongly fortified. Thus, the people might as well head back to Egypt because there was no way for the land to be taken. What would change their minds? Perhaps if they had a dozen stealth bombers, or a battery of missiles? Their position was, "God, we would believe You can take us in, if..." Unfortunately, this is not faith at all–it is a counterfeit.

The Genuine: Surrender Faith

Contract faith, the counterfeit, is putting the onus on God to perform before we are willing to put our trust in Him. Actually, it is acting as though we were God and He must do our bidding. That is not exactly the appropriate attitude of a finite creature toward the infinite Creator! We are the ones in need of God, not *vice versa*. We must come to God on God's terms, not on ours.

Furthermore, it implies that we don't think God can back up His Word, i.e., He isn't capable. But, if faith is as good as its object, and the object of Christian faith is Jesus Christ, the incarnate God, then whatever He says is the last word on any subject. Setting conditions is assuming that God has limitations. Surrender faith is not something I have to generate emotionally, nor is it confidence placed in a church. Surrender faith trusts unconditionally the infinitely powerful, wise, loving, and just God who created and sustains all that exists. What He says, He can and does do. If we know God that way, then the "commitment-making process based on the Word of God" is a very reasonable way to live. Instead of "I'll believe if..." it is rather, "I believe God, period."

The counterfeit and genuine faith mentalities are illustrated in turn by the Israeli spies sent into Canaan. The majority reported that, despite God's command and promise, a successful invasion of Palestine was not possible. The minority report by the remaining two spies, Joshua and Caleb, stated that since God had instructed them to take the land, they should proceed immediately to do so. What is the difference? Joshua and Caleb were basing their recommended action on a powerful and faithful God who had promised this land to them. No conditions could outweigh this single factor. But not so with the rest of the people. By following the majority report, they were indicating that other factors were more important in their consideration than God's Word. If those factors changed, they argued, then okay. Theirs was a contract with conditions, a counterfeit for faith. God's response to them underscores this point: "How long will these people treat Me with contempt? How long will they refuse to believe in Me, in spite of all the miraculous signs I have performed among them?"[7] The result was forty years of wilderness wanderings until Joshua and Caleb led the next generation into the promised land. The counterfeit of faith does not lead to relationship and fulfillment, but rather to disappointment and even unnecessary suffering.

The Illustration of Belief

The Roman Centurion

A Roman soldier made a statement which prompted Jesus to say to the multitude following Him: "I say to you, not even in Israel have I found such great faith."[8] What was there about the Centurion's faith which produced such glowing praise from Jesus?

The Centurion was a military officer who clearly understood authority. He had a favorite servant who was very sick and about to die. There is no indication that he had ever personally seen Jesus perform any miracles. Undoubtedly, he had heard stories of how Jesus had healed the sick, and therefore sent some Jewish friends to ask Him to come. When Jesus drew close to his home, the Centurion sent a message, "Lord, do not trouble yourself further, for I am not fit for You to come under my roof; for this reason I did not even consider myself worthy to come to You, but just say the word, and my servant will be healed."

The Centurion, humbling himself, expected Jesus to be able to heal his servant, even from a distance, thereby acknowledging His position of absolute authority over disease. He interjected no conditions. Rather, he simply asked Jesus to issue the command. This unconditional faith in the person of Jesus was really the recognition of His authority as deity, and prompted Jesus to commend him in glowing terms. The servant was healed and restored to good health.

Noah

There was a time when God grieved that He had made humankind because the earth was corrupt and filled with violence.[9] One man knew and served God faithfully–and "found favor in the eyes of the Lord." Noah was to be saved from God's judgment by riding out the coming worldwide flood in an ark. We do not know exactly where Noah lived, but it was unlikely on any seaboard. We can only imagine the scenario as God informed Noah of the coming deluge.

When instructed by God to build an ark, Noah had to wonder why such a boat would be needed–especially when God gave additional details. Noah was to make it 450 feet long (one-and-one-half city blocks!) 75 feet wide and 45 feet high, with three decks. From the time of God's instructions to the time of the flood was a period of 120 years. Noah worked to build this "ship" for much of that time. This gives new meaning to the concept of an avocation!

It is worth noting that Noah had three sons to help him. A study of the text, however, reveals that they were all born *after* the command to build. I can imagine how the family got started. After a few years of very slow progress on the ark, perhaps Noah came home discouraged. He may have commented to his wife that he didn't think he would ever finish building it. Perhaps, together, they hit upon a great idea: Shem. Two more good ideas quickly followed, that is Ham and Japheth. Now there were five who could work on the project.

It is a curiosity to wonder how Noah handled being a public spectacle in the community. His was certainly not an inconspicuous canoe. He couldn't hide it behind a bush. There was no escaping the fact that he was building a massive ship, likely not near a large enough body of water even to use it. It was probably with some regularity that the boys questioned Noah, "Dad, are you sure you heard that message right?"

The point of my conjectural narrative of this incident is that Noah's decision to build the ark was made strictly upon his acceptance of God, and, thereby on the authority of His Word. For nearly 120 years he was probably made the brunt of every joke for miles around. If I had been in his situation, I probably would have asked for a sign to keep up the faith (one-half inch of rain per day would have been encouraging). But not Noah: "Thus Noah did; according to all that God had commanded him, so he did."

> By faith Noah, being warned by God about things not yet seen, in reverence prepared an ark for the salvation of his household... and became an heir of the righteousness which is according to faith.[10]

By the time the ark was finished, it had already begun to rain. Water began to appear where it had never been before. The fool, Noah, began to look like a genius. His formula was really quite simple–he believed God unconditionally.

THE RESULTING IMPLICATIONS

Where Am I?

At times during my quest for spiritual certainty, I would end up thinking much like an agnostic. Maybe there were answers, but perhaps not–one could never know for sure. Faith is a personal thing, I thought: what works for some may not work for everyone. Reflecting upon those years from my current perspective, I believe this thinking stemmed from the ambiguity in my understanding. I had no clear distinction between the forms of unbelief, nor did I understand genuine versus counterfeit responses to God. If I had seen the options as I do now, I think I would have had a clearer focus and direction.

As I see it now, the first and central issue continues to be, "What position will we take in regard to Jesus Christ?" Our response to this question alone determines whether we are in the "unbelief" or "belief" section of Figure 3: Are we above the line or below it?

Have I placed my faith in Jesus Christ alone for my salvation?

Figure 3.

Our discussion of the faith triangle in Chapter 4 made clear the three basic reasons why our response may be "No."

1. Lack of Knowledge (ignorant unbelief): I do not know who Jesus is, what He said and did, nor the reasons for faith in Him.

2. Indecision (doubt): I have unanswered questions and apprehension about the implications for my life resulting in emotional uncertainty about what choice to make.

3. Willful Rejection (decisional unbelief): I live a decent life and deny that Jesus needed to die for me in order that I may go to heaven. I do not want to surrender to Him as Lord of my life.

On the other hand, to respond "Yes" would mean agreeing with the apostle Peter who said that "Christ died for sins once for all, the righteous for the unrighteous, to bring you to God."[11] It also would mean that we do what the apostle Paul said, that "...if you confess with your mouth, 'Jesus is Lord,' and believe in your heart that God raised Him from the dead, you will be saved."[12] The apostle John tells us what will result: "...to all who received Him, to those who believed in His name, He gave the right to become children of God..."[13]

Even if we say "Yes," we might view this faith relationship either as a contract with conditions, or as an unconditional surrender to God.

1. The Counterfeit: Contract "Faith": I give my life to God on the condition that He rewards me with health, wealth, heaven, etc. I have rights, make demands of God, and do good deeds to earn God's acceptance and special blessing.

2. The Genuine: Surrender Faith: I surrender my life unconditionally to God with repentance. I am accepted by His unconditional love and grace alone. I am motivated to do good deeds because of my love for Him, and enabled to do so by the inner power of the Holy Spirit.

In his book, *The Screwtape Letters*, C.S. Lewis created a series of letters from Screwtape, a professional devil and under-secretary of the department of temptation, to his nephew Wormwood, a junior tempter. Commenting on the greatest threat to the efforts of the devil in a human's life, Screwtape wrote:

Do not be deceived, Wormwood, our cause is never more in danger than when a human, no longer desiring, but still intending, to do our Enemy's will, looks around upon a universe from which every trace of Him seems to have vanished, and asks why he has been forsaken, and still obeys.[14]

This genuine faith is a trust which results from surrender to God because one has been persuaded by the evidence of who He is. It is not conditional on circumstances. Screwtape's description fits Jesus perfectly as He hung on the cross. He was not a victim–He chose to be there.[15]

And when circumstances turned dark, He still stayed there.[16]

What Difference Does It Make?

We have seen that the Christian faith is reasonable. The evidence for God seen through design in nature and the life of Jesus is conclusive. If it is true, we can believe in Him because of who He is, not for any rewards or benefits which may come to us. If He is real, then His

> "It is because...the religious view of the universe [in its Christian version] seems to me to cover more of the facts of experience than any other that I have been gradually led to embrace it..."
> C.E.M. Joad, *The Recovery of Belief*

presence in our lives has to make a difference. What does He promise will result from a genuine faith relationship with Him?

First, if I am in right relationship with God, then I am able to realize my human potential, i.e., become all that I was intended to be in this life. After all, if I want to know how a product can best be used, I go back to the manufacturer's instructions. Likewise, if God is my Creator, His specifications for my life should result in functional wholeness—intellectual, moral, and emotional completeness. Jesus said, "I have come that they may have life, and have it to the full."[17]

Second, if I am in right relationship with God, then I am able to realize my eternal destiny, i.e., to have assurance of life after death. Jesus said, "Let not your heart be troubled; believe ... in Me. In My Father's house are many dwelling places; ...I go to prepare a place for you ... I will come again, and receive you to Myself, that where I am, there you may be also."[18]

Can we boldly believe that Jesus is alive, coming to earth again in the future, and will take us to live in His presence forever? The apostle Peter warned there would be scoffers who say, "Where is this 'coming' He promised? Ever since our fathers died, everything goes on as it has since the beginning of creation."[19] He then reminds his readers that the people of Noah's day scoffed in the same way. But when the flood came, Noah looked like a genius—because he believed God, and lived by His Word.

Peter adds: "By the same word the present heavens and earth are reserved for fire, being kept for the day of judgment..." Why is Jesus so slow in keeping His promise to return? "He is patient with you, not wanting anyone to perish, but everyone to come to repentance."

I remember coming to the point in my life when I realized that I no longer had any major intellectual reasons keeping me from faith in Christ. But the effect of that realization was not what I expected. Instead of being eager to take that step, I was still holding back, being cautious. What was keeping me from letting go and allowing Jesus Christ to be in control of my life? Later I came to realize what it was–something very powerful and at the same time subtle. Only God was adequate to overcome the single most important factor that kept me from faith in Jesus Christ. When He did, I was surprised.

– FOCUS & DISCUSSION –

1. Which of the three forms of unbelief do you think is the most common? How might your answer vary for people in other countries of the world?

2. Assuming you were honestly seeking personal faith in Jesus Christ, is it important to know which form of unbelief you hold? Why?

3. Is it possible to mentally misjudge a person's unbelief or faith position based only upon first impressions? What is necessary to know for sure? What does this suggest about the importance of developing trusting relationships as a basis for discussing one's faith?

4. Sometimes we hear the expression, "Seeing is believing." Read 2 Peter 3:3-10. If a person followed the expression above, when would he/she believe in the second coming of Jesus Christ? What basis do Christians have for believing in the second coming of Jesus if not according to the expression above?

– DISCOVERIES –

The purpose of this chapter was to explain and clarify the meaning and life implications of the first eight "Ah-ha!" discoveries. Making sense of unbelief, doubt, and faith is important. Likewise, knowing the difference between a counterfeit and genuine faith can help us avoid future spiritual disappointment and pain.

Hopefully, this chapter has answered the question for you, "Where Am I?" While no new discoveries have been identified, exactly what you are accepting or rejecting in your own life should now be clear.

Ah-ha!

Discovery #8
New Relationship, Freedom, Hope

Discovery #7
Certain Object, Valid Faith

Discovery #6
Jesus Backed His Claim

Discovery #5
Jesus Claimed to be God

Discovery #4
Historically Reliable Records

Discovery #3
Eyewitness Records

Discovery #2
God Became Flesh

Discovery #1
No God? DEATH Wins

WHAT'S NEXT?

Are you willing to give God permission to miraculously transform you into a new person, and reform you more and more into the image of the Lord Jesus Christ? Hopefully and prayerfully your answer is "YES."

Sometimes people feel a reluctance in their spirit to take this step of faith. They are hesitant about the changes God wants to make in their life. In fact, the Bible identifies one particular factor which keeps more people from faith and the growth of faith than any other.

What is this stumbling block to faith and life transformation? We'll discover that in the last chapter.

CHAPTER 6

HOW CAN I KNOW GOD?

Recognizing the Stumbling Block
Taking the First Step

"It's Jesus. It's Jesus that changed my life.
I want everyone to know it's Jesus."
The late Payne Stewart, professional golfer, to Pastor J.B. Collingsworth,
after watching video from Stewart's 1999 U.S. Open victory.[1]

❧

"Only God changes hearts."
Paul Azinger, professional golfer, discussing the conversion of his friend,
Payne Stewart

❧

"You and I have a God-shaped vacuum at the center of our being."
Blaise Pascal, seventeenth century French physicist

S everal years ago I served as the academic dean of a small, Midwestern college. It was my job to interview candidates for faculty positions. I recall one candidate who was extremely likeable, but with limited education. I enjoyed his visit to our campus immensely, but knew I had to tell him he was not qualified for the job. After what seemed like an hour of oblique comments and nuances in my attempt to be diplomatic, the man looked at me and asked, "What's the bottom line?" In one sentence, in about five seconds, I then told him the unguarded truth.

A student who had attended one of my college classes called me unexpectedly from his home during the summer break. After exchanging greetings, he talked at great length about an opportunity that was open to him. He was very complimentary to me about what a wonderful person and professor I was. Finally, I had to ask, "What is the bottom line? Why are you calling?" He then admitted that he wanted $1,500 from me.

Years earlier, something similar to this had happened to me in my quest for God. I had spent many months interacting with numerous lines of excellent evidence. I had dialogued with several people. I weighed the pros and cons of a commitment to follow Jesus Christ. The time came when I had to ask the question, "What is the spiritual bottom line?" That question made me face up to the truth: It was no longer a series of legitimate intellectual questions keeping me from faith. I had to deal with something much more difficult–a spiritual factor inherent in the depths of my nature.

IDENTIFYING THE SPIRITUAL FACTOR

The spiritual factor can be identified in an incident from Peter's life, before he became a believer and apostle.

One day as Jesus was standing by the Lake of Gennesaret, with the people crowding around Him and listening to the Word of God, He saw at the water's edge two boats, left there by the fishermen, who were washing their nets. He got into one of the boats, the one belonging to Simon, and asked him to put out a little from shore. Then He sat down and taught the people from the boat.

When He had finished speaking, He said to Simon, "Put out into deep water, and let down the nets for a catch."

Simon answered, "Master, we've worked hard all night and haven't caught anything. But because you say so, I will let down the nets."

When they had done so, they caught such a large number of fish that their nets began to break. So they signaled their partners in the other boat to come and help them, and they came and filled both boats so full that they began to sink.

When Simon Peter saw this, he fell at Jesus' knees and said, "Go away from me, Lord; I am a sinful man!" For he and all his companions were astonished at the catch of fish they had taken...[2]

The Prerequisite to Faith

After fishing all night and catching nothing, Peter and his crew were washing the nets and probably eager to get some rest. Fishing was no weekend sport for Peter, but rather his vocation. He was experienced and surely knew in detail every feature of the lake. He had undoubtedly tried every technique he knew that night. The fish just were not biting, so to speak. He was probably disgusted and not in a very good mood.

In this setting, Jesus, the carpenter and itinerant religious teacher (and novice fisherman!) suggested dropping the nets in deep water. The event that followed is most instructive. Peter was clearly reluctant because he was confident he knew exactly what would happen (and besides catching no fish, it would mean washing the nets again). To avoid embarrassment with his crew, he made certain they knew that this was not his idea ("because you say so"). Peter thought he knew better than Jesus. This was his turf. On the beach, Peter was the "pro." Anyway, what would a traveling rabbi know about fishing? From this perspective, Peter addressed Jesus as "Master" or teacher, a title of respect but recognizing only His humanity.

Then came the astounding, massive catch of fish. Peter's response was significant. He identified himself as a "sinful man" and addressed Jesus as

Figure 1.

"Lord," meaning supreme in authority. The word he chose was "kurios," sometimes meaning simply "sir," but in most cases it is the translation of the Hebrew "Jehovah" or God. In view of Peter's sudden humility and his response of worship, it is clear he was attributing deity to Jesus.[3]

The spiritual factor can be seen more clearly by referring to Figure 1 (above). The upper and lower triangles within the rectangle represent Peter and Jesus, respectively. Before the miracle catch of fish, Peter was the "pro" and imagined he knew more than Jesus, particularly about fishing on the Sea of Galilee (illustrated by the large base of his triangle on the far left).

As the incident unfolds, illustrated by the "path to faith" diagonal from left to right, the upper triangle representing Peter becomes smaller, and the lower triangle representing Jesus becomes larger (illustrated by the large base of His triangle on the far right). The miracle revealed Peter's limitations and prideful independence. The result was his admission of sin and confession on his knees that Jesus is Lord. It was Peter's realization that Jesus is Lord which moved him from pride, the spiritual factor and stumbling block, to humility. This insight and brokenness often occurs along the path to a faith relationship with Jesus.

The Key to Usefulness

The illustration in Figure 1 has clear implications for our lives. Intellectually, we may be persuaded by the evidence that Jesus is the incarnation of God. Our self-sufficiency and pride may keep us from acknowledging that we need Him. As long as we believe we are the "pro," we will be unwilling to submit to Jesus' right as Lord to direct our lives. As Jesus said to the self-righteous and proud Pharisees, "It is not the healthy who need a doctor, but the sick. I have not come to call the righteous, but sinners to repentance."[4] That's why the Christian faith is not entered through works, but rather through forgiveness at the foot of the cross of Jesus.

In my own case, humility was not my strong suit. The spiritual factor of my pride was the greatest deterrent keeping me from faith and dependence on Jesus, that is, from kneeling at His feet. In order to follow Him in obedience, I needed to experience His forgiveness and submit my life to be dependent on the power given to me by His Spirit.

Illustrating the Spiritual Factor

It may be helpful to illustrate how this spiritual factor was reflected in the lives of John the Baptist and Moses, two people used by God in very significant roles.

John the Baptist

John the Baptist was six months older than Jesus and had lived a life of personal denial and singleness of mind. His whole life was a preparation to announce the coming of Jesus the Messiah, "the Lamb of God who takes away the sin of the world."[5] He had many disciples of his own, and a significant popularity. He had made great sacrifices for the success he was experiencing. It was easy for me to imagine him aggressively defending his right to his position and fame.

A few months later, John's followers came to him with an understandable concern: More people were beginning to follow Jesus than John. His followers had apparently become jealous and viewed Jesus' activities as an infringement on the rights of John. John saw it differently. He testified, "After me comes a Man who has a higher rank than I, for He existed before me ... the thong of whose sandal I am not worthy to untie."[6] In total humility he then declared, "A man can receive nothing, unless it has been given him from heaven ... He [Jesus] must increase, but I must decrease."[7]

How could John do it? Because he was in a faith relationship with God and knew that doing God's eternal will was more important than temporal position and success. In other words, he had learned humility. Such an attitude was eulogized by Jesus as He later spoke of John: "I tell you, among those born of women there is no one greater than John."[8] It would have been difficult for me in my college years to imagine my competitive nature being controlled and channeled in such a humble way.

Moses

Everyone who is acquainted with the feats of Moses in Egypt would view him as a giant among men. Few realize that his reputation is based entirely on the period in his life *after* he reached eighty years of age. In fact, as I will attempt to demonstrate, the operation of the spiritual factor identified above in his early life was the key to his later greatness.

Moses was born the son of slave parents in Egypt at a time when the Pharaoh had declared a death sentence on male Hebrew newborns.[9]

In a desperate move to save his life, his mother placed him in a basket in some reeds near the bank of the Nile behind the royal palace. Upon finding the crying child, Pharaoh's daughter felt pity and adopted Moses as her own son. By these providential circumstances Moses enjoyed the luxury and privilege of royalty for the first forty years of his life. He is described as being "educated in all the wisdom of the Egyptians and was powerful in speech and action." Without exception, he was the most educated and powerful Israelite in the world of his day.

At about the age of forty, Moses committed treason by killing an Egyptian guard out of sympathy for a Hebrew slave who was being beaten. He also attempted to be an arbitrator or judge in Hebrew disputes. The significance of these activities is found in Moses' perception of himself: "...he supposed that his brethren understood that God was granting them deliverance through him."[10] There is no biblical statement or even a hint that God had approached Moses to be His chosen deliverer at this time. God did approach him for this task forty years later—a critical delay for a very important reason.

It seems apparent that Moses had acted on his own. Why? He was the "big man" in the palace! However well intended, it is clear that he overestimated his own importance and impeccability. He was above the law, a benevolent autocrat. He was the "pro." Moses' pride led him to believe that if ever there was someone who had the power to save the Hebrews from their slavery, he was that person. But he was rebuffed by his own people, and to add insult to injury, his adopted Egyptian family pronounced a death sentence upon him. He had failed utterly, and ran for his life into the desert of modern Saudi Arabia, near the Gulf of Aqaba.

No competent vocational counselor would ever suggest a career of shepherding in the wilderness to the most educated and capable Israelite in the world. Only God could know how remedial a forty-year stint in the desert would be to a bad case of the spiritual factor: namely, self-sufficiency and pride. I can imagine how often Moses must have reflected on his failure, how badly he had "blown it." He had had it all—and lost it.

UNDERSTANDING TWO QUESTIONS

"Who Am I?"

Against this backdrop, after another forty years, God spoke to Moses from the midst of a "burning" bush in the desert. "Therefore, come now, and I will send you to Pharaoh, so that you may bring My people, the sons of Israel, out of Egypt."[11] Forty years earlier Moses might have thought, "God, I don't know you very well, but I have to hand it to you, you certainly know how to pick 'em. If anyone can do a job like that, I surely can." But at eighty years of age, after forty years in the wilderness, Moses responds, "Who am I, that I should go to Pharaoh, and that I should bring the sons of Israel out of Egypt?" This is a changed Moses, a man with humility. Besides, forty years earlier he already tried what God was asking and it hadn't worked. Why should it be any different now? Moses had not yet understood the significance of his own pivotal question, "Who Am I?"

God's response to Moses is critical to my thesis: "Certainly I will be with you ..." The implication is obvious. When Moses tried to save his people forty years earlier he had done it on his own, presumably because he thought he was quite adequate alone. That's why he failed. This time it wouldn't be the adequacy of Moses but the power of God working through him which would guarantee success. At forty, Moses was the most educated and capable Hebrew in the world, a man of pride, the "pro." At eighty, he was a humbled man recognizing his need for God in order to truly succeed in his life and activities.

"Who am I?" or better, "Who do I think I am?" was the first critical question I faced as my own spiritual bottom line. Reluctance to admit my moral failure and need–pride–was a greater deterrent to confessing faith in Jesus as Lord than any other single factor.

"God, Who Are You?"

Moses was still not sure. He had a painful memory which he carried for forty years, that is, the rebuff of his own people: "Who made you a ruler and judge over us?" they had asked. Fearing a repeat of this challenge, Moses asked, "God, who are you?" That is, "What is Your name, so I can tell them who sent me?" God's answer is awesome, "I Am Who I Am." Moses was to go as the instrument of God the "I Am," the One without beginning or end, the forever present tense, the Eternal One. Moses questioned further: "What if they will not believe me...?"[12] God proceeded to turn Moses' shepherd's crook into a snake and back again, and his hand leprous like snow and healed again. God was not dependent on Moses' education and capabilities. He has all the power in the universe. God made it clear to Moses that He is capable and desirous of filling yielded and humble human vessels with His love and power, so long as praise and credit were properly directed to the source of all goodness, to God Himself.

These are the two timeless questions each of us must face in mind and experience in coming to faith in Jesus Christ. In spite of our abilities, we must recognize that something is still missing from our lives. The paradox of power and humility which is evident in Moses' later life must be attractive to us. Moses was eulogized for "all the signs and wonders which the Lord sent him to perform in the land of Egypt against Pharaoh ... and for all the mighty power and for all the great terror ... he performed." Yet Moses was described as "very humble, more than any man who was on the face of the earth."[13] It is unlikely he learned this humility in the palace in Egypt. Perhaps everyone should consider a visit to the desert to learn shepherding.

APPLYING THE SPIRITUAL FACTOR

The two questions, "Who Am I?" and "God, Who Are You?" were not formalized in my thinking at the time I was struggling with my own faith commitment. But the concept was. I realized that who I thought I was determined to a great extent how big my God could be. I had come across this idea in my reading of C.S. Lewis.

> *"...One's relationship to God and to Jesus Christ is strictly a personal relationship... One cannot remain neutral about Him."*
> Charles Colson, former White House aide

In God you come up against something which is in every respect immeasurably superior to yourself. Unless you know God as that–and, therefore, know yourself as nothing in comparison–you do not know God at all. As long as you are proud you cannot know God.[14]

I was both hesitant and incapable of making myself smaller, so to speak. It was not until God revealed to me how big He is, that I finally saw myself small in comparison. It changed the course of my life.

Recounting My Assets

I was born and raised in a small farm community of southeast South Dakota. This setting was hardly the context from which arrogance is generated, though in jest we would express our pride that at least we were not from the neighboring state of Iowa!

There were many assets which I inherited from my parents, but two stand out as having had prime importance to me. In fact, they were so important to me that I allowed them to become liabilities. The first asset was that I had good athletic ability. In hindsight it is apparent to me that my world of comparison was not very large, but from where I stood then, I was "pretty good." Conference, regional, and state championships in various sports gave me a basis for thinking I was better than others. This was reinforced regularly by the press coverage I would get in our local newspaper, a weekly. Front-page news included the local high school gridiron or other sports highlights. The more ink I got, the more my ego grew. The coaches first noticed a problem when each week they had to issue me a larger football helmet!

The second asset which I turned into a personal liability was intellectual acumen. High marks came easily for me, and gained for me the reputation of being "smart." The recognition and awards I received in the academic area, added to my athletic achievements, were a formula for fueling my self-identity and values. At that point God was not important–I was doing fine without Him. I wasn't so much arrogant as I was self-sufficient and conceited.

During sophomore biology lab I met a girl who saw life differently. Vernee, too, was very capable, but talked about a personal relationship which she had with Jesus. This was her focal point in life, determining self-acceptance and values. She also had humility. I found her attractive and we began to spend time together. Her influence set me on a spiritual search which was several years in the making. It was also some years later that we married, and I have loved her, biology, and the Lord to whom she pointed me ever since! However, the years until then produced a spiritual bankruptcy which set me on that new course.

Temporal Prosperity

My attending college was assumed. Sorting out the scholarship offers and holding out for the best deal was a palace experience (a la Moses) making me feel I was in the driver's seat of my destiny. College years produced more athletic exploits, academic achievements, and even social recognition. I was even named the king of the Valentine ball on campus.

Intellectually I was most impressed with the logical and rational, yet personable, faculty I met in the natural sciences. They were not cowed from their scientific convictions about human evolution in the face of criticism from what I then viewed as less informed and narrow religious types. My choice of a degree in biology and secondary education contained a crusade element; that is, I would go out and rescue the next generation from religious narrow-mindedness to this more-enlightened, scientific understanding.

The height of my vanity as "the pro" came during my first year as a high school teacher of general science, biology, and chemistry. I received a telephone call from the chairman of a graduate biology program at a state university. He persuaded me to visit the university to become acquainted. But as I explained to him, the years of college with three varsity sports and a demanding science curriculum had left me tired. I wasn't immediately looking forward to graduate education. Nevertheless, I completed the application process, primarily because after teaching three months of general science to junior high school students, it was apparent to me that there were worse things than going back to school!

It was shortly after the Christmas holiday that I was called to my principal's office to receive a long-distance call. The same graduate school department chairman was calling to congratulate me on my acceptance to his biology department. He also informed me that I had been chosen as the recipient of a full-ride, national scholarship which would pay all educational expenses plus a stipend sufficient to live on for a four- to five-year Ph.D. program. I should have collapsed to my knees in tears of gratitude–but I didn't. I am embarrassed and ashamed to recall my thoughts as I headed back to my science laboratory: "When you're good enough, this kind of thing happens to you!" I imagined that I had earned that award. Instead of experiencing gratefulness, this was the ultimate ego-trip. I was going to be a Ph.D.!

Spiritual Bankruptcy

God must have had a good laugh, so to speak, over my pretension to have the world by the tail. Shortly after arriving at the university to begin graduate studies, I met some men–Christians–who did not fit my anti-intellectual stereotype. Some were even university Ph.D. scientists. None of them were pushy about their faith, but did defend it with evidences which I never knew existed. Particularly, I wondered how anyone could justify belief in a Bible that propagated such pre-science myths as special creation in six twenty-four-hour days, an actual hell (fire and all) and a real devil–to name a few. I knew better than that!

I don't recall any adversarial relationships with these men, but in my own heart I set out to prove I was right. I began to read books they gave me on external evidences such as archaeology and manuscript studies. It was a complete surprise to me that the New Testament writings were the most reliable of antiquity. Another man challenged me to read and critically study the New Testament writings firsthand. It was true that I had been acquainted with the Bible since I was a child, but I had not examined its truthfulness as an adult.

For the first time in my life I was applying the tools of evidence and reason to the investigation of faith. This educational process continued for months. I was spending as much time scrutinizing the Bible and books on evidence as I was on my graduate studies in biology. Little by little it dawned on me that I was wrong about almost everything on which my skepticism was based. The evidence about Christianity which I was learning had begun to satisfy my mind. But God was not close. I sensed no relationship there.

The interesting thing was that my reading kept bringing me back to focus on the person of Jesus. I was intrigued by Him–both attracted and repelled at the same time. I liked His life–compassionate, witty, sensitive, powerful, ethical, etc. But some of His teachings were threatening–absolute authority, uncompromising holiness, and unlimited forgiveness, even toward enemies. Secretly, like Peter the fishing "pro," I still thought these were some of the things which I knew better than Jesus.

My turning point came late one night in a most unexpected way. My wife Vernee had already gone to bed, leaving me alone to hit the books, as was my custom, into the wee hours of the morning. At some point I decided to read in the Bible for awhile. I don't recall why, but I was attracted to the Old Testament book of Job. Being competitive, I read with interest the challenge the devil presented to God concerning Job's life.[15] Reading the disaster that came to Job, I felt God was unfair and I agreed with Job when he cried out that "God has wronged me."[16] I felt he was perfectly justified to say, "Nevertheless I will argue my ways before Him... Behold now, I have prepared my case ... let me speak, then reply to me."[17] I believed God had some accounting to do. Who did He think He was anyway?

Job got his chance. I was as surprised as Job when God appeared and spoke to him: "Who is this that darkens My counsel with words without knowledge? Brace yourself like a man; I will question you, and you shall answer Me."[18] God spoke with tongue in cheek when He said He would sit at Job's feet so He could learn from him! It's not possible to feel the full impact of this encounter without reading it in its entirety in Job 38-42. Some excerpts of God's questioning will serve only to give the sense of it:

Where were you when I laid the earth's foundation? Tell Me if you understand. Who marked off its dimensions? Surely you know!...

Have you ever given orders to the morning, or shown the dawn its place...

Have the gates of death been shown to you?...

Can you bind the beautiful Pleiades? Can you loose the cords of Orion? Can you bring forth the constellations in their seasons...?

Who endowed the heart with wisdom or gave understanding to the mind?...

These were all questions about the precision and splendor of the universe. It occurred to me that God must truly be "into science." This is where I was good. These questions probed deeper into the mysteries of origins and functions than those in any exam I had ever taken. However, the best was yet to come: biology, my specialty.

Who provides food for the raven when its young cry out to God and wander about for lack of food?...

Who let the wild donkey go free? Who untied his ropes?...

Do you give the horse her strength or clothe his neck with a flowing mane?...

Does the hawk take flight by your wisdom and spread his wings toward the south? Does the eagle soar at your command and build his nest on high?

After two full chapters of scientific and intelligent design questions, God turned to Job and demanded: "Will the one who contends with the Almighty correct Him? Let him who accuses God answer Him!" Job's response was not what I expected: "I am unworthy–how can I reply to You? I put my hand over my mouth. I spoke once, but I have no answer–twice, but I will say no more."[19]

In my conceit, I thought Job's response was rather wimpy. Didn't he know anything about these matters? I did not yet see God as clearly as Job did.

God continued: "Would you discredit My justice? Would you condemn Me to justify yourself? Do you have an arm like God's, and can your voice thunder like His? ...Unleash the fury of your wrath, look at every proud man and bring him low ... Then I myself will admit to you that your own right hand can save you." What follows are two more chapters of questions concerning the order and design evident in the world.

Suddenly, in a profoundly personal way, God was no longer talking to Job–He was talking to me! Powerfully, though not audibly, I experienced the voice of God questioning, "Don, who do *you* think you are anyway?" My mind's eye flashed back to the many incidents of pride, envy, self-sufficiency, independence and conceit. God was revealing to me the true nature of my heart. In contrast to that, it seemed I was in the presence of a powerful, wise and righteous God. Job's final remarks described what I was experiencing:

I know that You can do all things; no plan of Yours can be thwarted.

You asked, "Who is this that obscures My counsel without knowledge?" Surely I spoke of things I did not understand, things too wonderful for me to know.

You said, "Listen now, and I will speak; I will question you, and you shall answer Me." My ears had heard of You but now my eyes have seen You. Therefore I despise myself and repent in dust and ashes.[20]

I slipped out of my chair to my knees and began to cry. A deep emotional thought possessed me: "Lord, I'm sorry!" Growing up, I had been conditioned to believe that strong people don't cry; that it was a sign of weakness in a man. That night machismo didn't matter. I was devastated by the conviction of my sinfulness, and I could only repeat again and again, "I'm sorry–Lord, I'm sorry." I am not certain how much time had lapsed before I was surprised by an unexpected development.

I was still on my knees reflecting on the awesomeness of God and my new desire to be under His authority. It began with the thought that I was free–of my need to win, to be number one, and to prove myself; of the slavery to my ego. I didn't have to perform any more. Oh, what a release! It was only then that I was flooded with the realization that I was forgiven. God's love through the sacrifice of Jesus, the Lamb of God, had paid it all. It was as if all the rules and regulations I had associated with church and God were gone. Figuratively, in their place was a caring, personal God with outstretched arms saying, "Don, I love you." I humbly had to admit my spiritual bankruptcy and accept forgiveness as His gift to me. Tears were flowing again, this time not of regret. They were tears of joy as my heart cried, "Thank you ... Lord, thank you ... thank you!" I was a new man—forgiven and free.

Under New Management

Many years have passed since that eventful night. I went on to complete that Ph.D. in biology, and later an M.A. in New Testament studies, but not for my ego. The reality of a personal relationship with Jesus, whom I now knew to be very much alive, instilled in me accountability to my Creator and ultimate Judge. It is not as harsh as that may sound—it is the right combination of love and discipline. I have been set free to serve, and to become more myself under His Lordship than ever before —the way I was created to be. I am at peace—under new management.

What difference has Jesus made in my life? Let me be specific.

1. **I have received and continue to experience the forgiveness of my sin.**

   He died once for the sins of all us guilty sinners, although He Himself was innocent of any sin at any time, that He might bring us safely home to God.[21]

   If we confess our sins, He is faithful and just and will forgive us our sins and purify us from all unrighteousness.[22]

2. **I have new life from above, am adopted into the family of God and enabled to follow Him by the Holy Spirit within me.**

   Yet to all who received Him, to those who believed in His name, He gave the right to become children of God...[23]

   "But the Counselor, the Holy Spirit, whom the Father will send in My name, will teach you all things and will remind you of everything I have said to you."[24]

3. I am at peace with God and do not fear judgment.

"For God did not send the Son into the world to judge the world, but that the world should be saved through Him. He who believes in Him is not judged..."[25]

There is therefore now no condemnation for those who are in Christ Jesus. For the law of the Spirit of life in Christ Jesus has set you free from the law of sin and of death.[26]

4. I have the assurance of eternal life after death.

"I am the resurrection and the life; he who believes in Me will live even if he dies..."[27]

These things I have written to you who believe in the name of the Son of God, in order that you may know that you have eternal life.[28]

It must be understood that I do not claim these because I consider myself worthy, or have done some deed to earn them. The Bible says, "Because of His kindness you have been saved through trusting Christ. And even trusting is not of yourselves; it too is a gift from God. Salvation is not a reward for the good we have done, so none of us can take any credit for it."[29]

My wife, Vernee, and I both recognize that we would not have stayed together in marriage for more than fifty years now if not for the grace to forgive and change–which comes from Him. Our two sons have come to acknowledge Jesus as Savior and Lord. There is great hope in knowing that when our family relationship here must end, death will only serve to reunite us once again, this time for all eternity. Every aspect of my life has been enriched under the new management of Jesus Christ.

> *"Following Jesus Christ has been an experience of increasing challenge, adventure and happiness. He is totally worthwhile. How true are His words: 'I am come that they might have life, and that they might have it more abundantly.'"*
> Mark Hatfield, former U.S. Senator from Oregon

A Personal Invitation

Clark Pinnock has expressed in a succinct way what I have personally discovered about faith in my life journey.

> I am convinced that faith needs to face up to the truth question and that the Christian message fits the facts. It is not a presupposition that has to be accepted on authority or a self-evident truth that needs no argument; it is a solid truth claim that can be tested and verified across the whole range of human experience. It meets our existential needs, makes sense out of our religious intuitions, stands up under rational scrutiny, corresponds with the historical evidence and speaks to today's moral necessities...

> To stand beneath the lordship of Christ is not a misfortune or humiliation for you. It is rather the entrance into abundant life and an existence that is truly desirable.

> Therefore, I make this appeal to you: open yourself up to God, confess your failure to live a just and holy life, and determine to follow the Lord Jesus. Act upon the evidence that stands before you and accept the saving offer that is being extended.[30]

The Bible says that Jesus came "to seek and to save that which was lost."[31] Jesus respects your will. He waits for an invitation—a commitment on your part to ask Him to forgive you and take the wheel. No one can say it better than He did.

> Come to Me, all you who are weary and burdened, and I will give you rest. Take My yoke upon you and learn from Me, for I am gentle and humble in heart, and you will find rest for your souls. For My yoke is easy and My burden is light.[32]

The apostle Paul promised that "if you confess with your mouth Jesus as Lord, and believe in your heart that God raised Him from the dead, you shall be saved..."[33]

These promises don't mean much until you reach out and take them for yourself. If you are sensing a desire to be in a relationship with God through faith in Jesus Christ, tell Him so through prayer. This simple prayer may be used if you are not sure what to say:

Dear God, thank you for providing us evidence for Your existence. I want to know the reality of a personal relationship with You. I acknowledge that my sin has separated me from You. I repent, and confess Jesus Christ as my Savior and Lord. I believe He died in my place and that you raised Him from the dead. Please give me the gift of the Holy Spirit to direct my life, and enable me to understand and follow Your Word from this day on. Thank You for adopting me as Your spiritual child and giving me the assurance of eternal life. Amen.

– Focus & Discussion –

1. It is stated in the text that a refusal to admit one's own identity as a sinner is a greater deterrent to recognizing Jesus' deity than any other single factor. Explain. Can you relate to this personally?

2. What two questions must each person ask and honestly answer along the path to personal faith? How are they related?

3. What is the "bottom line" in a person's getting right with God? Why is pride or self-sufficiency such a difficult thing to deal with? Is the difficulty primarily intellectual in nature?

4. What if someone said, "Becoming a Christian is the easiest thing in the world." What do you think they mean by that?

5. What does the fact that salvation is a gift imply about a Christian's basis for assurance of eternal life? What is it dependent upon?

— Discoveries —

The final two *FaithSearch* discoveries summarize Chapter 6:

9. Pride keeps more people from faith and forgiveness in Jesus Christ than any other factor!

10. I can experience a vital relationship with God, and the assurance of life after death, by a confession of faith in Jesus Christ through prayer!

Ah-ha!

Discovery #10
A Miracle of New Life

Discovery #9
Stumbling Block: Pride

Discovery #8
New Relationship, Freedom, Hope

Discovery #7
Certain Object, Valid Faith

Discovery #6
Jesus Backed His Claim

Discovery #5
Jesus Claimed to be God

Discovery #4
Historically Reliable Records

Discovery #3
Eyewitness Records

Discovery #2
God Became Flesh

Discovery #1
No God? DEATH Wins

What's Next?

Congratulations on completing your reading of *Surprised by Faith.* I hope it was helpful in your pursuit of knowing God, answering your questions about faith, or that it strengthened and deepened your existing faith. In whatever way God used it in your life, I invite you to take a very important next step toward greater spiritual fulfillment in the future. The Bible says,

> And now just as you trusted Christ to save you, trust Him, too, for each day's problems.... See that you go on growing in the Lord, and become strong and vigorous... (Colossians 2:6-7, TLB).

There is so much more awaiting you! Check out "Taking the Next Step" on the following page, and the resources for growth after that. Don't monopolize what you have learned, either. Share it with others. Help them also to make the discovery of faith in Jesus.

TAKING THE NEXT STEP

What happened in your life as a result of reading *Surprised by Faith*? I would like to hear about it. Use one of the communication means indicated below—it would be encouraging to me.

1. I have confessed my sin and prayed to follow Jesus as my Lord. Now what?

Your prayer of commitment to Jesus Christ is the most significant one you will ever make. Jesus made a promise to His followers when He said, "I came that they might have life, and might have it abundantly" (John 10:10). The difference between a "so-so" faith and the abundant life Jesus promised is found in building our relationship with God through the study of His Word, the Bible. I have written another book which will guide you in that meaningful and exciting process.

If you became a Christian–made a faith commitment to trust and follow Jesus Christ for the first time, as a result of reading *Surprised by Faith*, I want to provide you with a free copy of my Bible study book, *Growing Faith*. Please share your story of what happened when you call or write, and provide your name, mailing address, telephone, E-mail, and indicate your age as Jr. High or Sr. High, 19-35, 36-54 or 55+. Use one of the communication means indicated below.

Dr. Don Bierle
FaithSearch International
12701 Whitewater Dr., Suite #150
Minnetonka, MN 55343, U.S.A.
E-mail: sbf@faithsearch.org
Telephone: 952.401.4501

2. I have rededicated my life to follow Jesus as my Lord. Now what?

Regular study of the Bible will be the stimulus for you to grow spiritually. Put on the full armor of God to resist future temptation and spiritual attacks from your flesh and the devil (Ephesians 6).

I recommend that you purchase a copy of *Growing Faith*, or perhaps two (order online at shop.faithsearch.org) and go through it with a friend. Alternatively or in addition, order a copy of the *Surprised by Faith Study and Discussion Guide* for an indepth exploration of the ten *"Ah-ha!"*

discoveries identified in this book. It, too, will guide you in Bible study and answer many of the questions you may have about the Christian faith. I'm happy for you and stand ready to help in any way I can.

3. What if I have more questions or suggestions?

Good. I'd like to hear about them from you. Indeed, you may have objections or an evaluation concerning the contents of this book, or of the Christian faith. In any case, I invite your communication.

The subject of Jesus Christ is important enough to justify taking another step to resolve whatever questions or objections that may remain. Send me an E-mail or call the number above, whatever is most convenient for you. I look forward to hearing from you.

EVENTS BY DR. DON BIERLE

Dr. Don Bierle travels nationally and internationally to preach in worship services, to teach youth and adult education classes, to share at colleges and universities, and to present a wide array of evidence-based events. His animated and professionally prepared PowerPoint® slides make learning easy and the impact powerful. Contact his office using the address on the following page, for further information and scheduling.

FaithSearch Discovery: Discovering the *"Ah-ha!"* of Life

FaithSearch Discovery presents an inspiringly, breathtakingly logical case for believing in the historical person of Jesus Christ. Based on Dr. Bierle's book *Surprised by Faith*, this dynamic presentation is for everyone who wonders why they should believe, and for everyone who wonders why they do. *FaithSearch* Discovery has challenged, inspired and wonderfully changed hundreds of thousands of people, providing satisfying answers to life's important questions.

- Why am I here?
- Is Jesus really God?
- How can I know God?
- Is the Bible true?
- Can faith be reasonable?

FaithSearch Origins: *Making Sense of Creation & Evolution*

Biologist Donald A. Bierle, Ph.D., uses the Bible and current scientific evidence to unravel creation, evolution and the meaning of life. His emphasis on the powerful concept of Intelligent Design will unite rather than divide people on this controversial subject. Stimulating, challenging and biblically conservative, *FaithSearch* Origins is ideal for students, teachers, pastors, and parents.

FaithSearch Destiny: *Making Sense of Life after Death*

Using logic, and biblical and historical evidence, *FaithSearch* Destiny separates truth from fiction concerning the afterlife. This compelling presentation covers critical issues about the existence of God, the claims of reincarnation, the historical evidence for the resurrection of Jesus, fulfilled prophecy, and the end of the world. *Making Sense of Life after Death* provides answers to questions each person should resolve about the course of life... and death.

(Continued on Next Page)

Other Selected Event/Message Titles

Testimony: A Scientist's Journey from Skepticism to Faith

Revealing the Fingerprints of God

Do All Religious Roads Lead to God?

What's In a Name? The Uniqueness of Jesus

Crucifixion and the Cross of Christ

Think Like Jesus: Living a Biblical Worldview

To learn more about Dr. Bierle's events and resources, call or write:

FaithSearch International
12701 Whitewater Dr., STE 150, Minnetonka, MN 55343, USA
Ph: 952-401-4501 or 1-800-964-1447
E-mail: info@faithsearch.org
Or visit our Web site at **www.faithsearch.org**

What Others Are Saying

"Dr. Bierle is an engaging communicator and teacher. He patiently answered each question from the simplest, most basic query–to the skeptic's confrontation–to the anguished seeker's pleas for answers–to questions no one had satisfactorily answered before. His presentation is clear, thought-provoking and demands a response." *–Linda Damm, director of Christian growth, Knox Presbyterian Church (Minneapolis, MN)*

"The evidence you presented was profound. I've never heard the facts you presented. As a practicing engineer, this new knowledge means more than I can say." *–MB, Oro Valley, AZ*

"I've been an atheist for many years but this book has come closer than anything I've ever read to convincing me of the validity of Christianity." *–JB, Minneapolis, MN*

"*FaithSearch* International is making a significant contribution to the body of Christ. Dr. Bierle's **FaithSearch** [Discovery] event effectively evangelizes and disciples people. It has been very well received at Wooddale Church, and has added a new dimension to our evangelism ministry. I enthusiastically recommend it." *–Leith Anderson, president, National Association of Evangelicals; former senior pastor, Wooddale Church (Eden Prairie, MN)*

"**FaithSearch** Discovery was the best apologetic event I have ever been part of. Not only did Dr. Bierle share evidence that supports biblical faith in a systematic way, his visual presentation was the best I have seen bar none! I heartily recommend **FaithSearch** to any church seeking to strengthen the faith and witness of its members." *–Bob Wilbur, associate pastor, Christ Community Church, C&MA (Fort Myers, FL)*

"I've been asking myself many questions about my faith–and they were all answered." *– NP (Youth)*

"Very moving and informative. I learned more tonight than any other time in my life. I enjoyed it." *– KB, Illinois*

Resources by Dr. Don Bierle:

For additional titles and description details, visit our Web site:
www.faithsearch.org

Surprised by Faith Study and Discussion Guide

The *Study and Discussion Guide* is a thorough exploration of the material in *Surprised by Faith*, and is ideal for indepth study for individuals and small groups, or in a classroom setting. This resource, together with the Bible, helps you make the same ten *"Ah-ha!"* discoveries you would at a live **FaithSearch** Discovery presentation. Thirty-six of the most often asked questions about the Christian faith are answered throughout the text.

Related DVD: "Is the Bible True?" The live recording of the PowerPoint® presentation consists of two parts: 1) Testing New Testament Integrity; and 2) Testing New Testament Historical Reliability.

Related DVD: "Revealing the Fingerprints of God." This presentation with PowerPoint support highlights the evidence for God's existence from nature, from history and from the transformed life.

FaithSearch Participant Guide

The *FaithSearch Participant Guide* is the perfect companion to **FaithSearch** Discovery. It provides summary notes on the complete presentation, and includes thought-provoking questions (and answers), supporting material and suggestions for further study.

FaithSearch Origins:
Making Sense of Creation and Evolution

Scientist and former skeptic Dr. Don Bierle has authored a valuable resource capturing the content of his popular **FaithSearch** Origins event. *Making Sense of Creation and Evolution* is more than just a companion piece to the presentation, however. The text is full of insight and current scientific information, and includes useful references to books and Internet sites for further reading and research.

(Continued on Next Page)

Related DVD: "Making Sense of Creation and Evolution." The two-hour presentation with PowerPoint support consists of five parts: 1) Origins; 2) Intelligent Design; 3) Macroevolution/fossil evidence; 4) Biblical creation; and 5) Knowing the Creator.

FaithSearch Destiny: Making Sense of Life after Death

Designed to help people get the most from the *FaithSearch* Destiny event, Dr. Bierle has authored *Making Sense of Life after Death*. Easy to follow, this publication also includes a wealth of Scripture references for personal study. Like the presentation, it explains and outlines the way to a personal relationship with God and the basis for assurance of eternal life after death.

Related DVD: "Jesus' Resurrection: Hoax or History?" There is only one direct evidence for life after death: the bodily resurrection of Jesus Christ in history. Some have presented arguments in an attempt to refute its credibility. The PowerPoint-based presentation details the facts which document Jesus' resurrection as historical truth.

FaithSearch Discipleship: Growing Faith

This discipleship manual contains eight easy-to-follow lessons to help a person get firmly rooted in the truth of God's Word, the Bible. Each lesson is intellectually and spiritually challenging, leading the user through selected readings and key Scripture passages which help them understand what God has done and will do in their life.

Growing Faith includes daily Bible readings and focus questions, on topics such as the Holy Spirit, overcoming doubt and temptation, learning to pray, and the importance of fellowship in the church. (*Leader's Guide* also available.)

Related DVD: "Choosing to be a Bond-Servant." (A bonus presentation on the "Resurrection" DVD, above.) Christians are often described in Scripture as servants, or in some Bible translations, as slaves of Jesus Christ. The negative association in U.S. history of the word "slavery" with involuntary servitude and abuse, causes many believers to be uncomfortable with the concept. It is equally unattractive to outsiders. Understanding it the way God revealed it and the way first-century Jewish Christians received it, recasts the concept into the context of love and a joyful rededication of our lives to Him.

BIBLIOGRAPHY

This bibliography is only a selection of resources which the interested reader can turn to for additional information about topics addressed in this book. Those seeking more details about specific references in the text should consult the footnotes identified throughout the chapters. They list the sources used and usually give page numbers.

BOOKS

Archer, Gleason L. *Encyclopedia of Bible Difficulties*. Grand Rapids: Zondervan, 1982.

Barnett, Paul. *Is the New Testament Reliable?* Downers Grove, IL: InterVarsity Press, 1992.

Blaiklock, E.M. and R.K. Harrison, eds. *The New International Dictionary of Biblical Archaeology*. Grand Rapids: Zondervan, 1983.

Blomberg, Craig. *The Historical Reliability of the Gospels*. Downers Grove, IL: InterVarsity Press, 2007.

Bowman, Robert, Jr. *Why You Should Believe in the Trinity*. Grand Rapids: Baker, 1989.

Boyd, Gregory and Edward Boyd. *Letters From A Skeptic*. Wheaton, IL: Victor, 2008.

Bruce, F.F. *Jesus and Christian Origins Outside the New Testament*. Grand Rapids: Eerdmans, 1974.

Bruce, F.F. *The Canon of Scripture*. Downers Grove, IL: InterVarsity Press, 1988.

Bruce, F.F. *The New Testament Documents: Are They Reliable?* Downers Grove, IL: InterVarsity Press, 2003.

Comfort, Philip W. ed. *The Origin of the Bible*. Wheaton, IL: Tyndale House, 2013.

Craig, William Lane. *Knowing the Truth about the Resurrection*. Ann Arbor, Mich.: Servant Books, 1988.

Craig, William Lane. *The Son Rises: Historical Evidence for the Resurrection of Jesus*. Chicago: Moody Press, 2001.

Evans, Craig A. *Jesus and His World: The Archaeological Evidence*. Louisville, KT: Westminster John Knox Press, 2012.

Evans, Craig A. *Fabricating Jesus: How Modern Scholars Distort the Gospels*. Downers Grove, IL: InterVarsity Press, 2008.

Geisler, Norman and Ron Brooks. *When Skeptics Ask: A Handbook on Christian Evidences*. Wheaton, IL: Victor, 2013.

Geisler, Norman and Thomas Howe, *When Critics Ask: A Popular Handbook of Bible Difficulties*. Wheaton, IL: Victor, 1992.

Geisler, Norman and William Nix. *A General Introduction to the Bible*. Chicago: Moody Press, 1986.

Geivett, R. Douglas, and Gary Habermas, eds. *In Defense of Miracles*. Downers Grove, IL: InterVarsity Press, 1997.

Green, Michael. *Who Is This Jesus?* Vancouver, BC: Regent College Publishing, 2007.

Groothuis, Douglas. *Christian Apologetics. A Comprehensive Case for Biblical Faith*. Downers Grove, IL: InterVarsity Press, 2011.

Groothuis, Douglas. *Jesus in an Age of Controversy*. Eugene, Ore.: Wipf & Stock Publishers, 2002.

Groothuis, Douglas. *Revealing the New Age Jesus*. Downers Grove, IL: InterVarsity Press, 1990.

Habermas, Gary. *The Historical Jesus: Ancient Evidence for the Life of Christ*. Joplin, MO: College Press Publishing Company, 1996.

Habermas, Gary and Antony Flew. *Did Jesus Rise From the Dead? The Resurrection Debate*. San Francisco: Harper & Row, 1987.

Kaiser, Walter, Jr. *Hard Sayings of the Bible*. Downers Grove, IL: InterVarsity Press, 2009.

McDowell, Josh and Bill Wilson. *He Walked Among Us: Evidence for the Historical Jesus*. Nashville: Nelson, 1993.

McRay, John. *Archaeology and the New Testament*. Ada, MI: Baker Academic, 2008.

Nash, Ronald. *Is Jesus the Only Savior?* Grand Rapids: Zondervan, 1994.

Neill, Stephen. *Christian Faith & Other Faiths*. Downers Grove, IL: InterVarsity Press, 1984.

Price, Randall. *The Stones Cry Out*. Eugene, Ore.: Harvest House, 1997.

Sanders, John. *What About Those Who Have Never Heard?* Downers Grove, IL:InterVarsity Press, 1995.

Schaeffer, Francis. *Escape From Reason*. Downers Grove, IL: InterVarsity Press, 2007. Ch.7.

Schaeffer, Francis. *The God Who Is There*. Downers Grove, IL: InterVarsity Press, 1998. Sec.I, Chs.1,5; Sec.II, Chs.1,2,& 5; Sects.III,IV,& V.

Schaeffer, Francis. *He Is There and He Is Not Silent*. Wheaton, IL: Tyndale House, 2001.

Stevenson, Kenneth and Gary Habermas. *The Shroud and the Controversy*. Nashville: Nelson, 1989.

Strobel, Lee. *The Case for Christ*. Grand Rapids: Zondervan, 1998.

Strobel, Lee. *The Case for Faith*. Grand Rapids: Zondervan, 2000.

Strobel, Lee. *The Case for the Real Jesus*. Grand Rapids: Zondervan, 2009.

Wilkins, Michael J., and J.P. Moreland, eds. *Jesus under Fire*. Grand Rapids: Zondervan, 1995.

ARTICLES

Fine, Steven. "Why Bone Boxes?" *Biblical Archaeology Review* 27 (Sept./Oct. 2001).

Greenhut, Zvi. "Burial Cave of the Caiaphas Family." *Biblical Archaeology Review* 18 (Sept/Oct, 1992).

Jones, Clay. "The Bibliographical Test Updated." *Christian Research Journal* 35 (No. 03, 2012).

Lemaire, Andre. "Burial Box of James the Brother of Jesus." *Biblical Archaeology Review* 28 (Nov/Dec, 2002).

Lemonick, Michael D. "Are the Bible's Stories True?" *Time* 146 (December 18, 1995):62-70.

Shanks, Hershel ed., "New Analysis of the Crucified Man", *Biblical Archaeology Review* 11 (Nov/Dec, 1985).

Shanks, Hershel. "'Brother of Jesus' Inscription is Authentic!" *Biblical Archaeology Review* 38 (Jul/Aug, 2012)

Tzaferis, Vassilios, "Crucifixion—The Archaeological Evidence." *Biblical Archaeology Review* 9 (Jan/Feb 1985).

JOURNALS

Biblical Archaeology Review. P.O. Box 7026; Red Oak, IA 51591. Published quarterly.

Biblical Illustrator. Customer Service, One LifeWay Plaza, Nashville, TN 37234. Published quarterly.

Christian Research Journal. P.O. Box 500; San Juan Capistrano, CA 92693. Published quarterly.

NOTES

Chapter 1: Why Am I Here?

1. Clark Pinnock, *A Case for Faith* (Minneapolis: Bethany, 1980), p. 24.

2. John Lennon & Paul McCartney, "Nowhere Man" (Northern Songs Ltd., 1965), recorded on *Rubber Soul*.

3. Michael Cassidy, *Christianity for the Open-Minded* (Downers Grove, IL: InterVarsity Press, 1978), p. 12.

4. An ecologist would suggest that grass finds meaning in returning to the soil in a natural cycle of nutrients. But this requires death, the sacrifice of the individual, for some undemonstrated higher cause. We are concerned here with where natural laws came from and what meaning they have beyond finite existence.

5. Pinnock, p. 34.

6. Paul Little, *Know Why You Believe* (Downers Grove, IL: InterVarsity, 1988), p. 15.

7. Dr. Flew was an atheist for most of his life, including when he composed this parable. He converted to deism and acknowledgment of God's existence as a result of several years of debates with theistic scientists regarding whether the universe bears the marks of an intelligent origin. As a result of the evidence, he changed his position.

8. The existence of specified complexity in the natural world rules out chance as the source. Highly ordered structures like the DNA molecule and the finely tuned features of earth which make life possible are examples that demand an intelligent source. This is the first "clue" to everyone in the world that a personal Creator (God) exists. This is also the clear teaching of the Bible in Psalm 19:1-4 (NIV) and Romans 1:18-20. Natural revelation, however, can only reveal THAT a personal Creator exists, but cannot tell us WHO it is. The "Testable Strategy" presented in *Surprised by Faith* provides historical evidence both for the existence of a Creator, and "who" it is.

9. Francis A. Schaeffer, *The Complete Works of Francis A. Schaeffer: A Christian Worldview, vol. 1: A Christian View of Philosophy and Culture* (Westchester, IL: Crossway Books, 1982), pp. 101ff.

10. Michael D. Lemonick, "Are the Bible's Stories True?", *Time* 146 (December 18, 1995):62-70.

Chapter 2: Is The Bible True?

1. For this evidence, see F.F. Bruce, *Jesus and Christian Origins Outside the New Testament* (Grand Rapids, MI: Eerdmans, 1974); and Gary R. Habermas, *The Historical Jesus: Ancient Evidence for the Life of Christ* (Joplin, MO: College Press Publishing Company, Inc., 1996).

2. Lee Strobel, *The Case for Christ* (Grand Rapids, MI: Zondervan, 1998), p. 81.

3. Ann Landers, "Ann is Taken to Task for 'Pushing Religion,'" *Minneapolis Star and Tribune*, December 15, 1985.

4. Julius Caesar, *The Gallic Wars*, (Norwalk, CT: Easton Press, 1983).

5. See the following sources for information on the numbers of various manuscripts: Bruce Metzger, *Chapters in the History of New Testament Textual Criticism* (Grand Rapids, MI: Eerdmans, 1963), pp. 144-151; F.F. Bruce, *The New Testament Documents: Are They Reliable?* (Grand Rapids, MI: Eerdmans, 1990), pp. 14-15; and Norman Geisler and William Nix, *A General Introduction to the Bible* (Chicago: Moody Press, 1986), pp. 385-408.

6. Clay Jones, "The Bibliographical Test Updated," *Christian Research Journal*, Vol. 35, No. 03, 2012, pages 32-37. This is a very recent magazine article that has researched many original sources to get the current manuscript totals cited in the text.

7. Archaeologists and textual scholars count every manuscript that is found as "one" regardless of whether it includes part or all of the ancient work. Therefore, the manuscript numbers cited include not only complete manuscripts but also partials, even fragments, of the work.

8. Jones, p. 34, citing The Institute for New Testament Textual Research.

9. Jones, p. 34-36.

10. F.F. Bruce, *The Books and the Parchments* (Westwood, N.J.: Fleming H. Revell, 1963), p. 178.

11. Frederic Kenyon, *Our Bible and the Ancient Manuscripts* (New York: Harper & Brothers, 1941), p. 23.

12. Harold J. Greenlee, *Introduction to New Testament Textual Criticism*, rev. ed. (Peabody, MA: Hendrickson Publishers, 1999), p. 6.

13. Philip Comfort, "Texts and Manuscripts of the New Testament" in *The Origin of the Bible*, Philip Comfort, ed. (Wheaton, IL: Tyndale House Publishers, 1992), pp. 179, 193.

14. Paul Barnett, *Is the New Testament Reliable? A Look at the Historical Evidence* (Downers Grove, IL: InterVarsity Press, 1986), p. 39.

15. David Van Biema, "The Gospel Truth?" *Time* 147 (April 8, 1996): 52-60.

16. Daniel B. Wallace, Center for the Study of New Testament Manuscripts, News Archive, February 10, 2012.

17. Comfort, p. 180.

18. Frederic Kenyon, *The Bible and Modern Scholarship* (London: John Murray, 1948), p. 20.

19. Craig A. Evans, *Jesus and His World. The Archaeological Evidence* (Westminster John Knox Press, Louisville, Kentucky, 2012), p. 76.

20. Ibid.

21. Bruce, *The New Testament Documents: Are They Reliable?*, p. 15.

22. Metzger, *Chapters in the History of New Testament Textual Criticism*, pp. 144-151.

23. Geisler and Nix, p. 475.

24. Bruce, *The New Testament Documents: Are They Reliable?*, pp. 19-20.

25. Geisler and Nix, p. 431.

26. Bruce Metzger and Bart Ehrman, *The Text of the New Testament: Its Transmission, Corruption, and Restoration*, 4th ed. (New York: Oxford, 2005), p. 126.

27. Kenyon, *Our Bible and the Ancient Manuscripts*, p. 23.

28. Frederic Kenyon, *The Bible and Archaeology* (New York: Harper & Brothers, 1940), pp. 288f.

29. Luke 3:1-2a (NIV)

30. Bruce, *The New Testament Documents: Are They Reliable?*, p. 82.

31. David Van Biema, "The Brother of Jesus?", *Time* 160, (November 4, 2002):70.

32. Andre Lemaire, "Burial Box of James the Brother of Jesus", *Biblical Archaeology Review* 28 (Nov/Dec, 2002):24-33.

33. Matthew 13:55

34. Galatians 2:9; Acts 21:18

35. Hershel Shanks, "Cracks in James Bone Box Repaired," *Biblical Archaeology Review* 29 (Jan/Feb, 2003):20-25.

36. Hershel Shanks, "'Brother of Jesus' Inscription is Authentic!", *Biblical Archaeology Review* 38:04, Jul/Aug 2012.

37. Joe Nickell, "Bone (Box) of Contention: The James Ossuary," *Skeptical Inquirer* (March/April, 2003):19-22.

38. See Flavius Josephus, *Antiquities of the Jews* (Grand Rapids, MI: AP&A), book XVIII, ch. 3, paragraph 3, p. 379; and Bruce, *Jesus and Christian Origins Outside the New Testament*, p. 22.

39. Robert Bull, "Caesarea Maritima–The Search for Herod's City," *Biblical Archaeology Review* 8 (May/June, 1982):24-41.

40. Matthew 26:57

41. Zvi Greenhut, "Burial Cave of the Caiaphas Family," *Biblical Archaeology Review* 18 (Sept/Oct, 1992):28-36.

42. C.A. Evans, "Caiaphas Ossuary," in S.E. Porter and C.A. Evans, *Dictionary of New Testament Background*. A compendium of contemporary biblical scholarship, electronic ed. (Downers Grove, IL: InterVarsity, 2000).

43. Luke 2:1-2 (NIV)

44. Randall Price, *The Stones Cry Out: What Archaeology Reveals About the Bible* (Eugene, OR: Harvest House, 1997), p. 299.

45. Luke 3:23

46. Price, p. 299.

47. See both Paul L. Maier, *First Christmas* (San Francisco: Harper & Row, 1971), pp. 15-22; and Habermas, *Ancient Evidence for the Life of Jesus*, pp. 152-53.

48. "Capernaum – House of Peter", www.AllAboutArchaeology.org; www.ChristianAnswers.net/dictionary/capernaum; "Capernaum: The Church of the House of Peter," www.mfa.gov.il/MFA - search "Capernaum."

49. J.R. McRay, "Archaeology and the New Testament: 4. Jesus and His World," and B. Chilton and E. Yamauchi, "Synagogues: 4. Remains of Buildings," in Porter and Evans.

50. Luke 7:1-5

51. McRay, "Archaeology and the New Testament: 4. Jesus and His World," in Porter and Evans.

52. Luke 2:22

53. John 5:1-5

54. John 9:1-12

55. Luke 8:26-33. See also McRay, "Archaeology and the New Testament: 4. Jesus and His World," in Porter and Evans.

56. Vassilios Tzaferis, "Crucifixion—The Archaeological Evidence," *Biblical Archaeology Review* 9 (Jan/Feb 1985):44-53.

57. Hershel Shanks, ed., "New Analysis of the Crucified Man," *Biblical Archaeology Review* 11 (Nov/Dec, 1985):20-21.

58. Craig Evans. *Jesus and His World.* p. 123.

59. Tzaferis, p. 52.

60. John 19:32-33 (NIV)

61. Tzaferis, p. 53. Zias and Sekeles later published their opinion that in the case of this crucifixion victim, the leg bones may have been broken postmortem, rather than as a final coup de grâce. See "The Crucified Man from Giv'at ha-Mivtar: A Reappraisal," *Israel Exploration Journal*, Vol. 35, No. 1 (1985), pp. 22-27.

62. Acts 17:6. Politarchs is a transliteration from the original Greek and is usually translated to English as "city authorities" or "rulers" in our New Testaments.

63. McRay, "Archaeology and the New Testament: 5. The World of the Early Church," in Porter and Evans.

64. Bruce, *The New Testament Documents: Are They Reliable?*, p. 82.

65. William M Ramsay, *The Bearing of Recent Discovery on the Trustworthiness of the New Testament* (Grand Rapids, MI: Baker Book House, 1979 reprint), pp. 81, 222.

66. W.F. Albright, *The Archaeology of Palestine*, rev. ed. (Baltimore: Pelican Books, 1960), pp. 127f.

67. Millar Burrows, *What Mean These Stones?* (New York: Meridian Books, 1956), p. 1.

68. Nelson Glueck, *Rivers in the Desert: A history of the Negev* (Philadelphia: Jewish Publications Society of America, 1969), p. 31.

69. Kenyon, *The Bible and Archaeology*, p. 279.

70. K.A. Kitchen, *The Bible in its World* (Downers Grove, IL: InterVarsity Press, 1977), p. 132.

71. Acts 2:22-23, 32-33

72. Acts 2:41

73. Acts 26:26

74. Bruce, *The New Testament Documents: Are They Reliable?*, p. 46.

75. Julius Muller's critique of D.F. Strauss' theory that the Gospel accounts are mere legends has never been answered: "Most decidedly must a considerable interval of time be required for such a complete transformation of a whole history by popular tradition, when the series of legends are formed in the same territory where the heroes actually lived and wrought. Here one cannot imagine how such a series of legends could arise in an historical age, obtain universal respect, and supplant the historical recollection of the true character and connecting of their heroes' lives in the minds of the community, if eyewitnesses were still at hand, who could be questioned respecting the truth of the recorded marvels. Hence, legendary fiction, as it likes not the clear present time, but prefers the mysterious gloom of grey antiquity, is wont to seek a remoteness of age, along with that of space, and to remove its boldest and more rare and wonderful creations into a very remote and unknown land." Julius Muller, *The Theory of Myths, in its Application to the Gospel History, Examined and Confuted* (London: John Chapman, 1844), p. 26; in William Craig, *The Son Rises* (Chicago: Moody Press, 1981), p. 101.

76. A.N. Sherwin-White, *Roman Society and Roman Law in the New Testament*, (Oxford: Clarendon Press, 1963), p. 190.

77. A.N. Sherwin-White, cited in Pinnock, p. 77.

78. Bruce, *The New Testament Documents: Are They Reliable?*, p. 88.

79. Sidney Collett, *All About the Bible* (New York: Revell, 1934), pp. 62-63.

80. Sherwin-White, p. 189.

81. William Ramsay as cited in Norman Geisler and Thomas Howe, *When Critics Ask. A Popular Handbook on Bible Difficulties* (Wheaton, IL: Victor Books, 1992), p. 385.

82. C.S. Lewis, *Surprised by Joy* (London: Collins, 1955), pp. 178f, 182, 187f.

83. Frank Morison, *Who Moved the Stone?* (Grand Rapids: Zondervan, 1977 reprint), pp. 8-12.

Chapter 3: Is Jesus Really God?

1. Luke 2:52

2. See Luke 4:14-30.

3. Isaiah 61:1-2

4. It may be argued that Jesus' claim to be the Messiah would not necessarily be a claim of divinity. But in view of His challenge in Matthew 22:41-46, He undoubtedly intended it as a claim to be God as well. In Luke 4:18-19, Jesus quoted from Isaiah 61:1-2. According to the same Old Testament book (9:6), the Messiah was called, "Mighty God, Eternal Father." Jesus' certain familiarity with this latter passage would mean that His claim to be the Messiah was also a claim to be God.

5. John 4:25-26; Mark 8:27-30

6. See Matthew 22:41-46.

7. R.V.G. Tasker, *The Gospel According to St. Matthew* (Grand Rapids, MI: Eerdmans, 1978), p. 213. In the *Tyndale New Testament Commentaries*.

8. See John 8:53-59.

9. See Exodus 3:14.

10. See John 10:22-33.

11. See John 8:23-24.

12. See John 5:21; 10:27-28; 11:25-26.

13. See Matthew 28:18.

14. John 19:7

15. John W. Montgomery, *History and Christianity* (Minneapolis: Bethany, 1965), p. 63.

16. See Luke 5:17-26.

17. Luke 5:24-26

18. John 9:1-3

19. Based on Jesus' response to two tragedies of His day recorded in Luke 13:1-5, i.e., the murder of some Galileans by Pilate and the accidental death of eighteen people when a tower fell on them, it is clear that He did not teach that all consequences that occur in life are the result of our personal sin. He did say, however, that sin is so serious that it results in death. Since we have all sinned, He said that we are in need of repentance in order to be saved from death.

20. Luke 7:11-16

21. See Luke 8:22-25.

22. Matthew 7:28-29. See also John 4:14; 8:12; and 11:25 for examples.

23. John 10:37-38 (NIV)

24. Compare Luke 4:1-13 with Matthew 14:33; 28:17; and John 9:38.

25. Compare Matthew 4:10 with Deuteronomy 6:13.

26. Compare Matthew 21:15-16 with Psalm 8:2.

27. See Luke 4:33-36 and Matthew 12:24.

28. John 8:46 (NIV)

29. John 14:6

30. See Mark 10:45 with Psalm 49:7-9.

31. Luke 9:20 (NIV)

32. Jon A. Buell and O. Quentin Hyder, *Jesus: God, Ghost or Guru?* (Grand Rapids, MI: Zondervan, 1978), p. 102.

33. For example, see Matthew 16:21; 17:9; 26:32.

34. John 2:19

35. Michael Green, *Man Alive* (Downers Grove, IL: InterVarsity Press, 1968), pp. 53-54, as quoted in McDowell, p. 193-194.

36. Luke 24:11

37. John 19:39-40 (NIV)

38. John 20:4-8

39. John 20:24-29

40. Matthew 28:11-15

41. Paul L. Maier, *First Easter* (San Francisco: Harper and Row, 1973), p.120.

42. 1 Corinthians 15:5-6

43. C.H. Dodd, "The Appearances of the Risen Christ: A study in the form criticism of the Gospels," in *More New Testament Studies* (Manchester: U. of Manchester Press, 1968), p. 128.

44. Luke 24:39

45. Luke 24:41-43

46. See John 7:5, 1 Corinthians 15:7 and Acts 15:13.

47. For the apostle Paul's own testimony see Acts 9:1-22.

48. See Matthew 26:56, 69-75; John 20:19.

49. Gary Habermas, *The Resurrection of Jesus* (New York: University Press of America, 1984), p. 39.

50. J.N.D. Anderson, *The Evidence for the Resurrection* (Downers Grove, IL: InterVarsity Press, 1966), pp. 3-4.

51. C.S. Lewis, *Mere Christianity* (New York: Macmillan, 1952), pp. 55-56.

52. Edwin Yamauchi as quoted in Strobel, p. 90.

53. John 11:25-26

Chapter 4: Can Faith Be Reasonable?

1. See 1 Corinthians 15:12-19.

2. John 14:6

3. Acts 4:12

4. Acts 1:8, NLT

5. Luke 24:47

6. Romans 10:14-15

7. J.B. Phillips, *The New Testament in Modern English* (New York: Macmillan, 1958), Romans 10:17.

8. Acts 1:8 (NLT)

9. Romans 10:16-21 (NIV)

10. Matthew 21:28-32 (NIV)

11. James 2:17 (NIV)

12. Luke 6:46-49

13. See Genesis 15:1-6 and 22:1-19 for this discussion of Abraham.

14. Genesis 22:2

15. Hebrews 11:17-19 (NIV)

16. For evidence concerning this identification, see 2 Chronicles 3:1; 1 Chronicles 21:15-30; Book of Jubilees 18:13; Josephus (*Antiquities I*. xii. 1; VII. xiii. 4).

17. John 1:29

18. Galatians 3:6-9 (NIV)

19. See Romans 4:16-25 (NIV).

20. John 7:37-39 (NIV)

21. John 14:15-17, 23

22. 1 Corinthians 6:19 (NIV)

23. Ephesians 1:13-14 (NIV)

24. John 3:1-18

25. Bertrand Russell, *A History of Western Philosophy* (New York: Simon and Schuster, 1945).

26. Mark 7:20-23 (NIV)

27. G.K. Chesterton, *Orthodoxy* (Wheaton, IL: H. Shaw Publishers, 1994), pg. 11.

28. Ephesians 2:8-9 (NIV)

29. Romans 3:10-11

30. John 6:44

31. Titus 3:4-7 (NIV)

32. J. Gresham Machen, *The Christian Faith in the Modern World* (New York: The Macmillan Company, 1936).

33. Philippians 2:13 (NIV)

34. 1 John 5:11-13 (NIV)

35. John 3:16

36. Romans 6:23

37. McDowell, pp. 327-28.

38. John 14:1-3 (NIV)

39. See John 5:21-29 and 12:48.

40. Romans 8:1-2 (NIV)

Chapter 5: Where Am I?

1. Elizabeth Elliot, *Through Gates of Splendor* (New York: Harper, 1957).

2. Ephesians 4:18 (NIV)

3. 1 Timothy 1:13

4. For examples see Matthew 16:21; Mark 9:31; 10:32-34; John 2:19-22.

5. John 20:24-29 (NIV)

6. See Numbers 13 and 14.

7. Numbers 14:11 (NIV)

8. See Luke 7:2-10.

9. This discussion of Noah is based on the text in Genesis 6-8.

10. Hebrews 11:7

11. 1 Peter 3:18 (NIV)

12. Romans 10:9 (NIV)

13. John 1:12 (NIV)

14. C.S. Lewis, *The Screwtape Letters* (West Chicago: Lord and King Associates, 1976), p. 51.

15. See John 10:17-18; Mark 10:45; and Matthew 26:53.

16. See Matthew 26:47-56 and 27:38-54.

17. John 10:10 (NIV)

18. John 14:1-3

19. See 2 Peter 3:3-13 (NIV).

Chapter 6: How Can I Know God?

1. Quotes taken from *Sports Spectrum* Magazine, used by permission: Art Stricklin, "The Transformation," (March 2000):17,19; and Paul Azinger, "Only God Changes Hearts," (March 2000):20,21.

2. Luke 5:1-11 (NIV)

3. A similar response using the same Greek word "kurios" is given by Thomas in John 20:28.

4. Luke 5:31-32 (NIV)

5. For background on John the Baptist, see Mark 1:1-8; 6:14-32; Luke 1:13-17; 3:1-20.

6. John 1:26-30

7. John 3:26-30

8. Luke 7:28 (NIV)

9. For the biblical accounts of Moses' life see Exodus 2 and 3, and Acts 7:17-38.

10. Acts 7:25

11. See Exodus 3:10-22 for this historical event.

12. See Exodus 4:1-17.

13. See Deuteronomy 34:10-12 and Numbers 12:3 for this paradox.

14. C.S. Lewis, *Mere Christianity*, p. 111.

15. See Job 1 and 2.

16. Job 19:6-7

17. Job 13:15-22

18. Job 38:2-3 (NIV)

19. Job 40:1-5 (NIV)

20. Job 42:2-6 (NIV)

21. 1 Peter 3:18 (TLB)

22. 1 John 1:9 (NIV)

23. John 1:12 (NIV)

24. John 14:26 (NIV)

25. John 3:17-18

26. Romans 8:1-2

27. John 11:25

28. 1 John 5:13

29. Ephesians 2:8-9 (TLB)

30. Pinnock, pp. 119, 121-2.

31. Luke 19:10

32. Matthew 11:28-30 (NIV)

33. Romans 10:9